CHAD

CHAD

i CAN'T BE STOPPED

by Paul Daugherty

ORANGE FRAZER *PRESS*
Wilmington, Ohio

ISBN 1-933197-13-7

Copyright 2006 Paul Daugherty

Additional copies of *CHAD: i CAN'T BE STOPPED* may be ordered directly from:

Orange Frazer Press
P.O. Box 214
Wilmington, OH 45177

Telephone 1.800.852.9332 for price and shipping information.
Website: www.orangefrazer.com

Cover Photo: Robert Flischel
Cover design: Jeff Fulwiler
Photo credits: Jeff Swinger and the *Cincinnati Enquirer*
Bessie Mae Flowers and Paula Johnson (pages 16-17, 26, 44-45, 56-57, 82)
Charles Collins and Selina Howard of the Phenom Factory (pages 81, 83, 87, 91)
Coach Robert Taylor at Santa Monica College (pages 70-71)
The Romer Collection: Miami-Dade Public Library (page 37)
The Historical Museum of Southern Florida (pages 31 and 35)

Library of Congress Catalogue-in-Publication Data

Daugherty, Paul, 1957-
  Chad, i can't be stopped / by Paul Daugherty
    p. cm.
  Includes index.
  ISBN 1-933197-13-7
   1. Johnson, Chad, 1978- 2. Football players--United States--Biography. 3. Cincinnati
Bengals (Football team) I. Title.

GV939.J6125D38 2006
796.332092-dc22
[B]
                                                          2006048300

Printed in Canada

ACKNOWLEDGEMENTS

acknowledgements

I first approached Chad Johnson in July 2005 about doing this book. He said no immediately. This was training camp, and training camp was about getting his mind ready for the approaching six months of football. There would be no room in Johnson's head in July or August to discuss a book. "Come back to me in September," he said.

I did, he agreed, and every Tuesday morning for seventeen weeks, between the opening game in Cleveland and two days after the playoff loss to Pittsburgh, we met at Johnson's condominium near Eden Park. Our discussions covered everything from musical preferences to tastes in food. Mainly, we talked football. It's what Johnson knows best and trusts most.

When you spend as much time with Chad Johnson as I did, you discover two things: One, he is not, in most ways, who he seems to be and, two, his passion for football is his best friend and worst enemy, often at the same time.

This is a book about football, but also about where Johnson came from and, just as important, who he came from. As loquacious as he is discussing football and the joy he takes in playing it, Johnson is just as reserved talking about his life away from the game. For insight into Johnson beyond his touchdown celebrations, I am indebted to a small army of people who have touched Johnson's life, and he theirs.

At the top of that list is Johnson's maternal grandmother, Bessie Mae Flowers, who did the bulk of raising him. You can't know Chad without knowing Bessie. I spent an afternoon with her, in her home in

Miami, and left believing her story was as good as her grandson's. Her cooperation cannot be overstated. Johnson's mother Paula was of great help as well, not only as a valued source of information but as someone who put me in touch with other people who helped her son growing up. There is a lot of Paula in Chad.

Charles Collins was invaluable in helping me understand what makes Johnson run. Probably, no one understands the often mercurial Johnson better than Collins, his position coach at Santa Monica College and current off-season guru. Speaking of Santa Monica College, many thanks to the head coach there, Robert Taylor, who always answered my phone calls, even at ridiculous hours of the day; Craig Austin, Taylor's former offensive coordinator; and Johnson's SMC teammates, Dylen Smith, Steve Smith, and Eugene Sykes.

Thanks to those at Miami Beach High School: Jim Kroll, Rick DiVita, Dale Sims and George Thompson. Special thanks to Terrence "T-Dog" Craig, for escorting me around the area where Chad Johnson grew up. Thanks to Sam Johnson of the Liberty City Optimists youth football club, and to Tyrone Hilton of the Gwen Cherry Boys and Girls Club, for helping me understand Miami's passion for youth football.

Thanks to Dennis Erickson and Tom O'Brien. Thanks to Jon Kitna, whose professionalism rubbed off on Johnson. Thanks to Marvin Lewis, who truly cares about his players, and to Hue Jackson. Many thanks to Bob Bratkowski. Thanks to Carson Palmer, Willie Anderson, and T.J. Houshmandzadeh.

Special thanks to Jack Brennan of the Cincinnati Bengals, who allowed me access to the club's scrupulously maintained archive of newspaper stories on the Bengals, from the day the team began play. Thanks to the Bengals beat writers of the last fifteen years. Their work was distinguished, even as the team they covered often was not.

Thanks to Dr. Paul George, Miami historian and Florida International University professor, whose insight into Miami early in the 20th century proved invaluable. Thanks to David Halbertstam, whom I've never met, but whose work over the years inspired and informed me in this venture.

And thanks to Chad Johnson, whose talent knows no bounds. He can't be stopped. Certainly not by me.—*Paul Daugherty*

TABLE OF CONTENTS

PROLOGUE

$\mathcal{F}$rom the day in April 2001 when the Cincinnati Bengals drafted him, you knew there was something different about Chad Johnson. He wanted to be a Bengal, for one. That was very different. After ten years of serious losing, no one who had a choice wanted to be a Bengal. Chad Johnson was 13 years old in 1991, when Sam Wyche's last Bengals team went 3-13, kicking off a twelve-year run as one of the worst-performing sports franchises in history.

In the decade before Johnson came to Cincinnati, the Bengals had won 47 games and lost 113. They hadn't had a winning season. They'd changed coaches four times and started nine different quarterbacks. They'd missed badly on nearly every No. 1 draft pick. Cincinnati was universally regarded as the Siberia of the National Football League.

Naturally, when the Bengals took Chad Johnson in the second round of the 2001 draft, the 36th pick overall, he was delighted.

"I didn't want to go somewhere they were already winning. I wanted to be the reason we started winning," Johnson said, years later. "I had no problems being a Cincinnati Bengal."

Johnson was the start of something good. Something remarkable, given the unique abyss in which the Bengals franchise had dwelled. He was the first highly-drafted player in years to confess excitement about coming to Cincinnati. He began a trend, one furthered most obviously by Carson Palmer.

The Bengals took the University of Southern California quarterback number one overall in the 2003 draft. Given their track record in drafting very early in the first round—Dan "Big Daddy" Wilkinson and Ki-Jana Carter were first overall picks, Akili Smith was taken third overall, John Copeland fifth, David Klingler sixth—no one was overly optimistic about the Palmer pick. No one but Palmer himself, who repeated the Chad Johnson mantra of two years earlier. "I'm not here to be part of the problem," Palmer said. "I'm here to be part of the solution."

And so he was. Palmer and Johnson, and Coach Marvin Lewis, gave rise to a downcast football team and its beaten-down town that continues today. It all started in a little house in the Liberty City section of Miami on Draft Day 2001, where Chad Johnson sat, anxious and unsure, in his grandmother's bedroom. The first round had come and gone and his name had not been called.

It seemed as if the whole neighborhood were crowded into Bessie Mae Flowers' home on the corner of NW 44th Street and 11th Avenue. Football in Miami is seen as the preferred vehicle for youngsters driving toward a better life. The kids in Liberty City and the surrounding areas begin playing organized tackle football at age 4. You could win a national college championship with players just from the three south Florida counties, Dade, Broward and Palm Beach. When one of their own is raised in the program and succeeds, it's a win for everyone.

A few hundred people gathered at Flowers' house that day, to eat collard greens, macaroni and cheese, candied yams and baked chicken, and to watch on the rented big screen television when their local boy Chad got drafted. Only he didn't. Not right away. Nothing ever came easily for Johnson. Part of that was his fault, part was circumstance. It's just the way it was. Draft Day was no different.

Johnson's lackluster performance at the NFL's pre-draft combine had dropped him from the first round. Teams also were leery of Johnson's history: He'd spent just one year at a Division I school, Oregon State, after taking three years to make it through junior college.

"A one-year wonder," was what many NFL personnel people thought of Johnson, recalled Bengals offensive coordinator Bob Bratkowski. In the spring of 2001, the Bengals had just hired Bratkowski from the Pittsburgh Steelers, where he had been the wide receivers coach. While still a member of the Steelers staff, Bratkowski had served as a coach at the Senior Bowl, in Mobile, Alabama. Chad Johnson had been invited to the game. In his one year at Oregon State, Johnson had averaged almost 22 yards a catch and had two touchdown receptions in the Beavers' 41-9 win over Notre Dame in the Fiesta Bowl.

Johnson opened Bratkowski's eyes in Mobile. "There wasn't a guy playing in that game who could cover him. Not all week," Bratkowski recalled years later. The Bengals' newest employee soon would be sticking his neck out for a player who'd been anything but reliable over the years. "I took a chance, but I felt good enough to stand up for him."

It helped that Bratkowski had spent twelve years as an assistant coach to Dennis Erickson, Johnson's coach at Oregon State. Erickson's appraisal of Johnson was similar to any coach's who had ever spent more than one practice with the immensely talented yet easily-distracted wide receiver: "He has all the raw talent you could want," Erickson told Bratkowski. "Putting it all together is the issue."

In Mobile, Bratkowski saw a player crazy about football. Then, as now, Johnson was sweetly candid, almost to the point of naivete. He told Bratkowski, "I don't drink, I don't smoke, I don't do drugs. I love football, I can't stand school."

"I kind of appreciated the honesty," the coach recalled.

Bratkowski also saw a player who was disappointed when practice ended, who couldn't get enough of the game. That was a trait that would endure through his first several seasons in Cincinnati.

"Tell Coach LeBeau I need more work," Johnson would say to Bratkowski, when Dick LeBeau was the Bengals head coach. "Tell Marvin (Lewis) let's go five more plays."

Chad Johnson was the only regular who volunteered to play on the scout team in practice, the only player who asked to play special teams.

Bratkowski fought hard for Johnson during the Bengals pre-draft meetings. "I said, this was a guy who could give us something we didn't have here: An ability to change a game, and to win one-on-one matchups," the coach explained, many years later.

Cincinnati had had a history of bottom-feeding, picking troubled players such as Carl Pickens and Corey Dillon in the second round, where they could pay them less money than a first-rounder, while hoping to get first-round results. Hoping, too, that the issues that dropped them out of Round One wouldn't persist.

Pickens and Dillon came to Cincinnati with reputations as great players of questionable character. History would show both assessments were accurate. Chad Johnson had no off-field problems. As Bob Bratkowski said, "The only reservation was his maturity. It was never an issue of him being a bad guy. It was self-discipline."

Bratkowski sold the Bengals on Johnson, but the team had bigger needs than wide receiver. The previous year, their defense had allowed 359 points, partly because the defensive line didn't mount an effective pass rush. Plus, they'd taken a wide receiver in the first round of the 2000 draft, Peter Warrick of Florida State. With the fourth pick in the first round, Cincinnati chose Justin Smith, a defensive end from Missouri.

In Liberty City, Chad Johnson slipped away from the party in his grandmother's living room, to watch the draft alone in her bedroom. "As players started going ahead of him, he couldn't handle it emotionally," says Charles Collins, Johnson's junior college position coach, longtime mentor and one of his closest friends. "His insecurity kicked in."

Over the years, lots of people would dismiss Chad Johnson, from teachers frustrated with his inattention—and absence—in class, to coaches taxed by his sometimes casual attitude. All mistook his easy-going nature for a lack of purpose.

As Johnson's friend and mentor Terrence Craig would put it, years later, "He didn't have a rough life, but a lot of people gave up on him."

Draft Day seemed just another example of that. Then the Bengals took a chance on him, and all was right. "I thought I was going to be a first-round pick," Johnson said, years later. "I wasn't disappointed, though. I just knew some way it would work itself out."

Johnson emerged to a roomful of hugs and tears. "It was like somebody took the chokehold off his neck and let him breathe," Charles Collins recalled.

"Coach C, we made it," Johnson said to Collins.

Even now, he recalls every wide receiver selected ahead of him that year: "Reggie Wayne, Santana Moss, Chris Chambers, David Terrell, Koren Robinson and Quincy Morgan. It was just another motivation. They didn't draft me? Make 'em pay. Most of those guys are doing pretty well, but I've been the most consistent."

During his first interview with the Cincinnati media, by phone on Draft Day, Johnson said, "I just want to tell the Bengals organization that I won't let you down." Years later, he would reflect on the day and say, "I was so happy. All that struggling, and I was there. I said, 'I'm going to make Cincinnati my city,'" Johnson remembered. "'I'm going to give those people something they haven't had for years.'"

Johnson was confident or prophetic, or both. The first player in a decade who wanted to come to Cincinnati was, as he'd promised, part of the solution. It hasn't been without incident, though. On the football field, Johnson has never done anything quietly.

—Paul Daugherty, spring, 2006

CHAD

This book will be about exploding myths and adding to legend, so let's start with a myth: Cincinnati Bengals wide receiver Chad Johnson never put his position coach Hue Jackson in a headlock. The playoff-game loss to the Pittsburgh Steelers was a distant if still painful memory for Jackson when he said this in February 2006, about the supposed halftime fight: "If Chad Johnson ever put me in a headlock, I'd beat him half silly." He would, too. Jackson is a lifetime hardass, minted on the gang-tough streets of south central Los Angeles.

The locker-room incident happened, and it didn't. Like a lot of the talk that swirls around Chad Johnson, it's somewhat true and somewhat not. A problem with being a star in the media and on the field is, occasionally you will be portrayed as someone you really aren't.

Chad Johnson, as we will see, is not prone to fisticuffs.

HAD

He is a mama's boy. Actually, a grandmama's boy. He is not an egomaniac or an exhibitionist. Off the field, he's practically reticent. He owns a ten-bedroom home in south Florida, not more than an hour from where he grew up. It's not quite finished, though, so he still spends the off-season in his grandmother's small house in Miami's Liberty City neighborhood, sleeping in the same bedroom he slept in as a child.

The locker room incident in the Pittsburgh playoff game happened, and it didn't. The only indisputable thing about it is this: You can't know Chad Johnson without understanding what occurred, and why, in that messy, chaotic, in-shock dressing room during those ten dramatic halftime minutes. Everything you love and hate about Johnson was on display, as obvious as the IV needle and tube hanging from his arm.

Johnson sat on a training room table, IV in place, taking fluids. This was a normal halftime activity for him, especially on warm days. January 8, 2006, was unseasonably warm in Cincinnati, with highs in the 60s, and Johnson was agitated to the point of anger. Most of the Bengals were. None showed it like Johnson.

"If Chad Johnson ever put me in a headlock, I'd beat him half silly."

On Cincinnati's second offensive play, a Pittsburgh defensive lineman named Kimo Von Oelhoffen had run into Bengals quarterback Carson Palmer. The low, late hit tore two ligaments in Palmer's left knee, the anterior cruciate, and the medial collateral. There would be considerable debate in the coming weeks over Von Oelhoffen's intentions. Now, there was only time to try to regroup.

The Bengals led 17-14 at halftime, but Pittsburgh had scored

There were better days versus the Steelers, such as going into Heinz Field mid-season and sending the Steel City into a month-long funk before the Good Ship Cowher righted.

a touchdown late in the second quarter. With Palmer's season over, a sense of inevitability hung over Paul Brown Stadium as the Bengals trotted into the locker room.

Chad Johnson had been antsy all week. The hype of the Cincinnati Bengals' first playoff game in fifteen years was getting to him. Johnson's mentor and confidante Charles Collins, his position coach when the pair were at Santa Monica (California) College, had gotten calls during the week from Bengals receivers coach Hue Jackson and wideout T.J. Houshmandzadeh. Both asked Collins to come to town, to calm Johnson.

"Chad's not focused," Collins recalls Houshmandzadeh saying.

"Speak to your son," Jackson asked Collins. It was not an unfamiliar request. Other than Bengals head coach Marvin Lewis, no one on the team was closer to Johnson than Hue Jackson. But Jackson's influence was not as strong as Charles Collins', whom Johnson credits for saving his football life.

Johnson's maternal grandmother, Bessie Mae Flowers, might have raised him to be a man. Collins was Johnson's football father. Collins flew to Cincinnati from his home in Los Angeles, hoping to soothe his star pupil. "He was a little nervous," Collins recalled, months later. "He would never admit it, but I know him."

On the sideline before the game, Collins told Johnson, "Focus. Be patient. Let the game come to you. Play it one down at a time, and don't worry about the game plan. That's Brat's job," Collins said, a reference to Bengals offensive coordinator Bob Bratkowski.

Johnson had always listened to Collins. From the time the pair formed an unlikely alliance in Los Angeles in 1998—Collins the teacher, Johnson the pupil whose lack of classroom work had cost him a year of college eligibility—Chad Johnson took as gospel whatever Charles Collins said.

Two years later, when a depressed Johnson called Collins from Oregon State, a week after arriving as a transfer from Santa Monica, he cried into the phone. "I want to come back. It's boring here," Johnson had said.

"I don't give a fuck," was Collins' reply. "If you even think about coming back here, I'm going to come up there and kick your ass. All the time I spent with you. The favor I'm asking Erickson to give you a chance," Collins said, a reference to his friend Dennis Erickson, then the Oregon State coach. Collins told Johnson returning to Los Angeles would not be an option.

"You're not going to embarrass me," Collins told Johnson.

Years later, Johnson would credit that phone call for keeping his football-playing dreams on course. It wasn't the first time "Coach C", as Johnson calls Collins, would play the fatherly, bad-cop role. And it wouldn't be the last.

The Bengals locker room at halftime of the playoff game had the feel of a hospital emergency room after a natural disaster. On one end of the room, closest to the training room, offensive coordinator Bob Bratkowski gathered the Carson Palmer-less offense. Bratkowski sketched plays on a greaseboard, twenty wondering men seated on wooden stools before him. Much of the second-half plan involved backup quarterback Jon Kitna throwing the ball more, specifically to Johnson, in part because Pittsburgh's defense would be anticipating more of a running attack, with Palmer out.

At one point, Bratkowski said to Hue Jackson, "Make sure Chad knows what I'm saying." Jackson went into the training room. Johnson was inconsolable. He'd caught just two passes in the first half, which, in his mind, hadn't helped the Bengals at all. Johnson's passion for football, and his belief he can carry his team by himself, has fueled him ever since he took up the game, at age 4.

"Chad's passion is always skewed by this: He thinks he can carry his team on his back," Jackson said. "His medicine is the ball. Giving him the football is a shot of energy. Not the media, not his teammates. The ball. That's who he is. That's his core. You never want to take that away from him."

Sometimes viewed as selfish, Johnson has never complained about his role in games the Bengals have won. It's only after losses, when he believes he could have done more to help the team win, that Johnson has unleashed his immaturity.

It wasn't often his frustration spilled over before a game ended. But this was no ordinary game. The Bengals had been the worst team in the National Football League for twelve seasons, between 1991 and 2002, the year Marvin Lewis was hired, compiling a bag-wearing record of 55 wins and 137 losses and amassing a comedy routine's worth of punch lines regarding the ineptitude. Playing for the Bengals was a sentence. Rooting for them was life without parole.

No wonder, then, that Lewis was seen as a savior. It took him three years to change the team's fortunes. In 2005, he'd coached them to the AFC North division title, and a first-round playoff game at home. Cincinnati treated this first playoff game since 1990 with all the pomp of a royal wedding. The *Cincinnati Enquirer* put out three special sections the week before the game, each beating the drum louder than the last.

"Let's Play" was the front-page headline of the final section, the morning of the game.

All week, players talked as if this game would define their season. Either they didn't realize what they'd already done for a city sick with losing, or it didn't matter. "We need to still exorcise some demons," offensive tackle Willie Anderson said during the week. "If we're going to get over the hump, it needs to be by beating Pittsburgh."

Johnson strayed from his norm, turning away media. "Marvin asked us to give something up for the team," Johnson announced. "I'm giving up talking."

Lewis made his players practice in pads that Wednesday, the first time in five weeks he'd ordered that. Lewis knew the game would be punishingly physical. He likened the game to a brawl: "We're going into an alley and only one team gets to come out."

Johnson had said that Tuesday, "I can't wait until Sunday." If his mood didn't indicate Johnson was already feeling the hype— he sat in the living room of his condo near Eden Park watching a

DVD of the musical *West Side Story*—his words did. "The offense is going to be ridiculous. It's going to be kamikaze out there, all or nothing."

Johnson said he wasn't watching *West Side Story*, with its story line of Sharks-versus-Jets gang violence, because of Lewis' remarks. Johnson just likes musicals.

"We're going to win," Johnson said that day. "I'm not guaranteeing it, but it's our turn. There's a reason why we made it this far. We're going to take it, then we're going to Denver next week (to play the AFC West-champion Broncos). I can feel it. I don't know what it is. I've been right about this stuff ever since training camp."

Johnson had, in fact, told Marvin Lewis as early as May, during a mini-camp, "This is our year." Lewis, who is usually more amused by his star wideout's exuberance than bothered by it, simply smiled and said "something about everyone doing their jobs," Johnson said.

"They (the Steelers) aren't going to be able to stop our offense," Johnson continued. "All we have to do is stop the run. And if they can't run the ball, it's over."

He pondered spending that Tuesday night at the stadium, with the coaches. Lewis himself had a pillow under his desk. "I'll be right there with them. I'll be sleeping in the lounge," said Johnson. He'd done that regularly in previous years, watching tape of the Bengals' next opponent so late in the evening, he dozed off. He stopped doing that when the team began supplying him with DVDs, which he'd take home to watch on the fifty-two-inch TV in his condo.

But that didn't mean Johnson stopped coming to the coaches' offices on Tuesday nights. That was the night they put in game plans. Johnson delighted in hanging around Bratkowski, offering

his suggestions, which invariably involved getting the ball
to Number 85.

His passion for football is such that Johnson hates Tuesdays
during the season. Tuesday is the players' only day off. Most
players relished the day away from the grind. Chad Johnson
dreaded the boredom. After he'd been to McDonald's for
breakfast, and to F.Y.E. to buy the newest CD and DVD releases,
he had nothing to do but play video games and make the
occasional paid appearance. Johnson much preferred every other
day of the week.

If you spent ten minutes with Johnson, you'd leave believing
the '05 Bengals were the '85 Bears. His enthusiasm was infectious,
his mood contagious. Even now, as Hue Jackson entered the
training room at halftime to deliver Bob Bratkowski's message,
Johnson's dour demeanor could infect his mates.

"There's a few things we're going to try in the second half,"
Jackson said to Johnson. Jackson's implication was clear: Calm
down, we're going to get you the ball. Just as clearly, Johnson
didn't believe Jackson.

"Coach, we're not going to try them," Johnson said.

"Yes, we are," said Jackson.

Johnson still didn't believe his position coach.

"OK," said Jackson, "you need to go tell Brat how you feel,
if you don't believe me."

Johnson bolted from the table, the IV still stuck in his arm.

"He comes out the training room door, the first person he sees
is Marvin," Jackson said. Johnson said to Lewis, "Coach, I need
the ball more."

There were at least ten people in the training room. By the
time Johnson reached the door, a few had grabbed him. He flailed
his arms, trying to free himself. "He never took a swing at Marvin.

He never put me in a headlock. We're two people he respects as much as anyone in the world," Hue Jackson said.

From over his shoulder, Bob Bratkowski heard the commotion. He turned and stared. Bratkowski had seen Johnson erupt before. This was nothing new. What was new was the atmosphere of a playoff game and the emotion of losing your star quarterback.

"Brat, forget about him" Bratkowski recalls an offensive lineman telling him. "Don't listen to anything he says."

Charles Collins had not intervened.

He'd seen this Chad Johnson many times, but not since his days at Santa Monica College. Hue Jackson had asked Collins to talk to Johnson during the first half, after Palmer went

"His medicine is the ball," said Chad's position coach, Hue Jackson. "Giving him the football is a shot of energy."

down, when both men realized Johnson's head was not in the game. Collins declined. "It's not my place," he said.

"After the first or second series, I knew what kind of game Chad was going to have," Collins said months later. "After Carson went down, the energy of the team went down. I said right away they had to get Chad involved, put him in a situation where he had to stay mentally in the game, from a physical standpoint.

"I'd have challenged him: 'Chad Johnson, you're a leader on this team. Step up.'" As it was, Johnson wasn't getting the ball and didn't feel as if he were part of the game. His quarterback was out, the Steelers had scored near the end of the half. Halftime wouldn't be pretty.

"He was in the tank," said Collins. "Hue just let him vent. They'd let it get too far away from them for him to bounce back mentally."

The first pass Jon Kitna threw to Johnson in the second half, Johnson dropped.

The halftime incident was not as it had been reported. Johnson had erupted, but he hadn't hit anyone nor put anyone in a headlock. Johnson isn't that kind of person.

"A big baby," Jackson has called him.

Bratkowski and Jackson were concerned about Johnson's mental well-being for the second half, but not about his tantrum. As Bratkowski would say nearly three months later, "It was a big deal, but there was business at hand. If it had been after the game, it would have been a bigger deal. As it was, we said, 'We haven't got time for that. We have a game to win.'"

Bratkowski kept his emotions chained for two days. The heat of the moment kept him thinking football, not histrionics. It wasn't until Tuesday evening after the game, when the coach happened to turn on the TV in his kitchen, that the emotions spilled out.

"His passion is a good thing and a bad thing. He has to learn to control it,
to make himself better and his team better. Separate the 'me'
from the team."——Bob Bratkowski

"Chad was on TV, giving a press conference," Bratkowski said. Johnson had called a local TV sportscaster and asked him to alert the Cincinnati media that he would be holding a press conference at Paul Brown Stadium, to explain his side of the incident. The Bengals didn't sanction it—"We don't respond to rumors," team public relations chief Jack Brennan said—so Johnson stood in the tunnel of Paul Brown Stadium, between the locker room and the field.

While admitting he was emotional, and his emotions got the best of him, Johnson denied anything had happened. "Ridiculous," he called it. "That sounds like drama. Nothing happened."

Later, Johnson worried what the incident might do to his reputation, in and out of town. "This one rumor can mess up everything positive I've done here. The face of this team outside this city is Chad Johnson. I know that everything I do personally is under a microscope. That's why I've never had a problem, on or off the field.

"Even though it's not going to jail or getting a DUI, it still reflects badly on me. No one is going to mess up what I have going on here, what I've meant for this city."

At home, watching the press gathering, Bob Bratkowski felt his blood pressure rise. "I went ballistic. I told my wife, 'I have to take a walk. My head's going to blow off.'" He left Johnson a pointed message on his cell phone, telling the wide receiver how disappointed he was in him, how he'd let down his teammates and himself. Johnson called back almost immediately. Too angry to answer, Bratkowski let it ring.

"We're going to have a man-to-man talk soon," Bratkowski said several months later. "It's all about this team. The thing that bothered me most was, it was halftime. We had the lead, and he was out of it mentally. Great players don't allow that to happen.

His passion is a good thing and a bad thing. He has to learn to control it, to make himself better and his team better. Separate the 'me' from the team. Every great player on great teams has had that ability."

Johnson wonders about his passion. Intellectually, he understands that great players channel their feelings. They make their emotions work for them. They don't blow up at halftime of the most important game of the year. He doesn't know how to change that part of himself, or even if he should.

On the Wednesday after the game, Johnson said, "How do you do that? I don't know. It would almost be like not caring. If you love this game the way I love it, that's why I'm so emotional."

Said Marvin Lewis, "He wants to compete and prove he's the best. I didn't say win."

More than anything, Chad Johnson wants to be a great football player. He wants to be remembered as the greatest wide receiver of all time. It's a wild ambition, but not out of the question, if he channels all that passion in the proper direction. It's a message delivered to him his whole life.

Starting first with his grandmother, the force of nature that is Bessie Mae Flowers.

BESSIE MAE

"*C*had, boy, what are you doing?"

The little boy in his Sunday best—white suit, knee-high white socks, white shoes—was sitting in a pile of construction mess. The little house at the corner of NW 44th Street and 11th Avenue, in the Liberty City section of Miami, was undergoing a bit of interior redecoration. Dust was everywhere, most prominently in the corner of the front room where 2-year-old Chad Johnson happened to be sitting.

Not ten minutes earlier, his grandmother, Bessie Mae Flowers, had said to her grandson, "Don't get yourself in that mess. You just stay right there while Mommy gets dressed." Naturally, Chad found the biggest pile of dirt and tested it.

"Mommy, look at me," he said.

That's when she knew. Bessie Mae would be reminded of that instant thousands of times over the next twenty years. She still recalls it, whenever she sees her grandson celebrate in the end

MAKE ROOM FOR CHAD——CHAD WITH GRANDPARENTS, IN GRADE SCHOOL, AND KINDERGARTEN.

zone or talk into a sideline camera. Occasionally, she'll leave him a message on his cell phone after watching an end zone romp she deems inappropriate. She'll tell him to read a specific Bible verse, often dealing with humility.

Chad has always been Chad, from that day he sat in the dust, dirtying his suit just before he was supposed to go to church. He was never bad, not in a malicious way. He was always mischievous. "That day was the first time I realized he was devilish," Bessie Mae said, twenty-six years later. "He is what we would consider a clown."

"Did you skip a class, Chad?" "No, Mommy. I just had to go to the bathroom."

He was born January 9, 1978. He and his mother lived with Bessie and her husband, James Flowers, in the Liberty City home Bessie had bought in 1964. Five years after Chad's birth, Paula Johnson would move from her mother's home to Los Angeles, taking with her Chad's 18-month-old brother, Chauncey, and leaving Chad with Bessie.

Paula recalls 5-year-old Chad, just inside the screen door of Bessie's house, as she left with Chauncey in her arms. "Bye, baby," she said. "I'll call you."

Paula Johnson wanted Chad to have the sort of childhood Bessie had provided for her. Bessie had used her savings from her teaching job to pay for the house, partly because she wanted Paula to have a yard to play in.

"I was an only child. I had whatever I wanted," Paula Johnson recalled. "I just wanted Chad to have all I had." Working part-time and temporary jobs in Miami wouldn't be enough, she figured. "I couldn't afford what my mom could. So why be selfish?"

"I'm leaving you here with everything you need," Paula recalled telling Chad that day. The little boy just stared. "I know you're OK here. I don't know what I'm going to do. Why would I take you?"

All Paula Johnson knew was her life in Miami was going nowhere. She needed a new start, especially after Chauncey was born. "Two kids out of wedlock. That's not me," she would say, years later. "I just couldn't get it together." The memory still pains her. "I do regret leaving him," she says. "But I did the right thing."

Paula Johnson spent three days with Chauncey on a Greyhound bus, Miami to Los Angeles. She got a job two days after she arrived, as a word processor in a law firm. Not long after, she added a second job, selling women's clothing in a department store.

After staying a few months with a family friend, Paula and Chauncey moved into an efficiency. Three years later, she moved to a two-bedroom apartment in Baldwin Hills, west of downtown Los Angeles, where she lived for fifteen years before moving to New York.

Paula and Chad Johnson bridged the distance as best they could. Chad spent summers and holidays in L.A. They talked on the phone almost every night. Paula's telephone bills topped $700 a month. "We did homework on the phone," she said. "I'd do papers for him and mail them to Miami.

"I still mothered. I knew what the homework was. I knew the teachers. I got reports. Even though I wasn't there, I was involved in everything. No decisions were made without my input."

She'd send cards, never forgetting a holiday. Easter. Halloween. St. Patrick's Day. Paula would send an extra card, for Chad to fill out and send to Chauncey. When he got to Los Angeles for the summer, one of the first things he and Paula did was color Easter eggs.

Chad even lived in Los Angeles for two years, as a sixth- and seventh-grader. Several years later, Bessie would kick Chad out of her house and command him to live with Paula. "Don't make it seem like I deserted him," Paula said recently. "The bottom line is, I'm still his Mommy." But the ultimate responsibility for devilish Chad rested with Bessie Mae. She was equal to the task.

For forty-two years, she'd taught English and reading in the Miami area public schools, everything from kindergarten to eighth grade. "I stayed until I got tired," Flowers recalled. "I didn't tell anyone I was leaving. I just went to the school board and filled out the retirement papers."

Students feared her, respected her and often dreaded being assigned to her classroom. "The word got around," said Flowers.

"Who you got for English?"

"Miz Flowers."

"Man, you better get outta there. That woman is crazy."

She enjoyed the little children the most. They were uninhibited and open to her teaching. They hadn't learned how to act out. The first few days of school, she'd ask the kindergartners and first-graders to write something about themselves. They'd fuss and complain about how they couldn't do it, didn't know what to say. But they complied. At the end of the year, Flowers would show them those first papers. The delight the children felt at seeing how much they'd improved was part of what pushed Bessie to get out of bed every morning.

Flowers' students understood quickly their teacher was not someone to be messed with. She learned to command attention by speaking in a low voice. They'd have to strain to hear what she was saying. They certainly couldn't yell. She understood from her

own childhood that following through was everything.
Miz Flowers meant what she said. She was not to be ignored.

"I just told them what to expect, and that was that. Here are
the consequences if you don't cooperate: First time, I call your
mother. Second time, I call the principal. Third time, you're
suspended for three days."

Years later, after he'd been kicked out of a junior college in
Oklahoma, she would send her grandson Chad away as well,
to teach him his actions had consequences.

Students late for class wouldn't be allowed in without an
admit slip from the office.

"Aw, man," they'd say.

To which Flowers might reply, "I'm not a man. I'm a woman.
Don't come in here to play, because I'm not playing."

The middle-schoolers caused more problems. Knowing Flowers'
reputation, school administrators often assigned the hard-headed
kids to her class. "The little devils nobody wanted, they dumped
on me," was how Flowers put it. She dealt with them, too.

A favorite trick of English students who hadn't read a book
she assigned was to claim they'd misplaced it.

"I lost my novel, Miz Flowers," they'd say.

"Really," Flowers answered. "I lost your grade."

"I would just say to them, 'We have rules in here. You can't be
coming in late, you can't be in my class with your pants all falling
down. Put a rope around your waist. I don't want to be seein' your
underwear, hear me?'"

It almost seemed as if a lifetime of dealing with unruly students
prepared her for her grandson. It wasn't that Chad Johnson was
unruly. There wasn't a mean bone in him. He just couldn't sit still,
didn't like school, and loved to play the clown. Anyone who has
watched him preen in the end zone understands that completely.

As she had done with Paula, Bessie Mae made sure Chad did not attend school in their Liberty City neighborhood. "I wasn't going to leave him over here," she said recently. "Chad was easily influenced, and we had some real incorrigibles around here."

Bessie had bought the house at 44th Street and 11th Avenue in 1964, moving her daughter from the asphalt of Overtown to the south, near downtown, to the small, grassy front yards of Liberty City, in Miami's northwest quadrant. Bessie wasn't alone. Tens of thousands of blacks already had moved from Overtown and its environs, either by choice or necessity.

Tourists visiting Miami today would hear of Liberty City only if they were being advised to stay away. The only thing Liberty City has in common with Miami Beach is heat. It began in the 1930s as Liberty Square, and it was described then as the most beautiful housing project in Florida. "Many people from Overtown saw this as heaven," explained Miami historian Dr. Paul George, a history professor at Miami Dade College.

Liberty Square was the brainchild of a white developer named Floyd Davis, as a means of easing congestion among the black population in Overtown. Laborers from all over the South, as well as from the Caribbean, had settled in Overtown, which at its founding near the turn of the 20th century was known as Nigger Town. There were jobs in Miami for blacks, fields to be worked, a railroad to be built. This caused housing demand—and prices—to rise beyond the means of most black families.

Davis' solution was to build northwest of downtown thirty-four single-family homes with electricity, gas and hot water. Each came with a yard and a garden. Lest anyone believe the scene idyllic, Liberty Square was encircled by a six-foot-high stone wall, a bludgeonous reminder to blacks of their station in the city.

As the black population expanded, so did Liberty Square.

Then in the late 1960s, federal highway officials decided Interstate 95 required a new exit ramp. Over the objections of residents, they ran it right through Overtown. It opened in 1971, displacing thousands of African-American families and countless businesses.

This occurred not long after Bessie Mae Flowers had decided to leave Overtown. She was ahead of much of the exodus. The resentment followed her, though. So did the riots of the 1980s and the gang warfare of the 1990s.

In 1980, thirteen people died in a riot in Liberty City after an all-white jury acquitted officers accused of clubbing to death Arthur McDuffie, a 32-year-old black insurance salesman they'd pulled over on a traffic stop. Nine years later, after a similar incident, Overtown and Liberty City erupted again, during the week before the 1989 Super Bowl, being held in Miami.

Driving today through the residential areas of Liberty City, marked as they are by small, tidy one-story homes, you aren't struck with a sense of fear. The area's business district has its share of boarded-up storefronts. You could say the same about the main drag in almost any Rust Belt town.

But where there is poverty, there are drugs and crime and people you want to keep your children from. That is why Bessie Mae Flowers made certain her daughter—and later her grandson, Chad—would be exposed to those influences as little as possible.

"Chad was always driven out of the neighborhood and that environment," Paula Johnson recalls. "My parents drove him at least forty-five minutes to school."

Bessie rode herd on Chad. She mother-henned him to the extent he couldn't leave the house on Saturdays until he finished his chores. He did his laundry, cleaned his room and put away his toys.

She'd drive him to school. Miami Lakes, North Miami Beach

Elementary, Coral Gables, Miami Beach High. Miles from Jackson High School and Northwestern High, the two schools serving Liberty City.

On the days she didn't drive Chad, he'd catch the bus. She recalls when Chad was at Miami Beach High that he frequently missed the school bus. Beach High started earlier than Nautilus Middle School, where Bessie taught, so when Chad missed the bus Bessie, still in her bathrobe, would load him in her car and chase the bus.

"Every time the bus stopped, I'd be right behind it, laying on the horn," she said. "Only way he'd get to school on time."

Her vigil extended to sports. Until he played football for the Liberty City Optimists as an eighth-grader, Johnson never took part in any organized games in the neighborhood. Bessie drove him to Pop Warner football games all over Dade and Broward counties and occasionally as far as Palm Beach, more than fifty miles north.

Saturdays in the late summer and throughout the fall, Bessie and her husband James drove Chad all over south Florida, to play kids' football. When they became lost, they just started looking for ball field light towers.

"I took him to school, I picked him up. Took him to football practice, waited there until it was done, then took him home. Every Saturday was a game, every Sunday was church," Bessie said. There was no time for her grandson to get with the "incorrigibles."

The kid from the 'hood, the NFL star with the twenty-four-karat-gold smile, the gold chains, and the tricked-out automobiles? He didn't learn any of that living at Bessie Mae Flowers' house. To her, her grandson might as well have been Beaver Cleaver.

Except for the clowning. Even at that, Chad Johnson was no worse than Eddie Haskell.

By the time he reached ninth grade, Chad was enrolled at
Coral Gables High, a predominantly white, middle- and upper
middle-class school. Bessie was at Nautilus in Miami Beach,
twelve miles away. The distance quickly became an issue.

Chad had a problem going to class. When he was supposed
to be there, he was anywhere but: In the bathroom (no child
ever used the facilities, or asked to use them, as much as Chad
Johnson), walking the halls, taking part in a gym class in which
he wasn't enrolled. A few years later, after Bessie had transferred
him to Miami Beach High, no one could find Chad anywhere.
Someone finally located him outside, with a crew of painters
contracted to paint the exterior of the school.

Every day, Bessie would walk to the office at Nautilus during
her free period, to pick up the inevitable pink message slips,
detailing calls from Coral Gables about her wayward grandson.

She'd pick up the phone and call Coral Gables High.

"Miz Flowers?"

"Ye-e-e-s."

"Your child won't come to class on time. It seems as if he even
skipped a class."

"What would you suggest I do? Would you like me to take him
to school with me? I'm at Nautilus. It's a middle school. Chad's
in high school. You might have heard."

Invariably, Flowers would make the twelve-mile trip to Coral
Gables, to the counselor's office.

"We need to talk about Chad."

"Yes," Flowers would answer. "That's why I'm here."

"What do you think we should do?"

"Give him a detention," Flowers answered. "Can I go now?"

Chad lasted a semester at Coral Gables, before Bessie pulled
him out and enrolled him at Beach High. If she were going to

receive daily summonses from the office at Beach, at least it wouldn't be much of a trip. Beach was three blocks from Nautilus Middle School.

Chad was Chad at Beach, too.

"A little butterfly, just flittering all over the place," Bessie said.

He'd always had an excess amount of energy. Bessie insisted he attend church every Sunday. She'd been raised by Bahamian immigrants who believed all any of us could depend on was the providence of the Lord. Bessie took that to heart. Problem was, Paula Johnson had her son baptized as a Catholic; Bessie was Baptist.

While Bessie attended Mt. Olivette Baptist Church in Overtown, Chad went with a neighbor to St. Francis. The two churches were eight blocks apart. Catholic Mass always ended before

Chad's first windsprints: From the Catholic Church to Bessie's Baptists.

the Baptist service, so Chad would run the eight blocks for the end of the Baptist doings. He preferred the high-energy music and singing in the Baptist church. More than two decades later, he still attends Mt. Olivette occasionally, when he is in Miami.

Too much energy has always been a theme. Years later, when he was living with Paula in Los Angeles and attending Santa Monica College, Chad would run to and from work and friends' houses. "Everywhere that child went, he ran," Paula recalled. "He ran to work. Half a mile. He ran home. Sometimes, I'd pick him and his brother up at a friend's house, after I got off work. Chad wouldn't get in the car.

"He'd race us home, about a quarter mile, down a steep hill. He'd win. It was like he was running for his life."

Soon enough, he would be. Now, he was cutting up at Beach High, running around, never where he was supposed to be.

"Miz Flowers?"

"Ye-e-e-s?"

Said Flowers, "He was upstairs when he was supposed to be down. He was the only child at Beach who had to pee four times a day." Beach High had a timeout room of sorts. They called it CSI, Class of Special Instruction, run by a man named George Thompson. Chad was its star pupil.

"He was a comedian," said Thompson. "That's what he was. That's what he is." Thompson remembers Johnson slapping students upside their heads, and running. He remembers him pulling chairs out from under students as they were sitting down, and tying their shoelaces together as they napped through a history lecture.

"He'd hide in places you didn't think he'd be," Thompson said. "Under cars, behind bushes. He'd never be disrespectful. It was always 'Yessir' and 'No, sir' with Chad."

He was a real cut-up. Then Bessie showed up.

"He'd be meek like a little lamb," Thompson said.

"Chad, what are you in CSI for?" Bessie would ask.

"They said I skipped a class, Mommy."

"Did you skip a class, Chad?"

"No, Mommy. I just had to go to the bathroom."

At that point, Thompson might interject, "He just wanted to go out in the hall and see who was there."

"But Mommy, I really had to go to the bathroom," Chad would protest.

Bessie would put an end to it. At least for a day. "Then wet your clothes and see what happens," she'd say, before returning to her other job, at Nautilus, the job she got paid to do.

After awhile, it stopped being funny. Johnson's lack of interest in school was reflected in his grades, which were consistently poor. He wouldn't graduate from Beach with his class. Johnson had to go to summer night school just to get his diploma, so he could be eligible to enroll in junior college and pursue his only love, football.

It was a pattern that would be repeated at Santa Monica College, where Johnson took three years to complete a two-year program. Even with the extra year, he needed to pass a class in summer school before he could be admitted to Oregon State. What should have been a two-year stay at a big-time school, where pro scouts would watch him play regularly, turned into barely a one-year NFL audition, in which he needed a spectacular photo-finish in the Fiesta Bowl and the Senior Bowl, just to merit a serious professional look.

Years later, Johnson would lament his disdain for academics. "I wasted a whole year (at Santa Monica) trying to get my grades together. If I could go back, I'd do it different. It would have saved me so much time. I'm glad it wasn't too late, but I did everything the hard way. My grandmother's way for me was so much easier, but I didn't see it that way."

The only thing that commanded Johnson's full attention was football. "No matter what, when it came time for him to play football, he was ready," recalled Rick DiVita, then an assistant coach at Beach, now the school's head coach.

Even then, Johnson saw football as something more than something to do on the weekends. Like a lot of kids growing up in Liberty City, he saw it as a point of neighborhood pride, a rite of manly passage, a way out. In Liberty City, football was never just a game.

Growing up, Johnson might not have had his mother around, or even known who his father was. He didn't have school to keep him straight. All he had for sure, day in and day out, was Bessie Mae Flowers. And football. He always had football.

BLACK MIAMI

"Oh ye of little faith, why art thou so fearful?"

Marian Cooper quoted Scripture. She had Scripture for every occasion. She needed it: Marian raised eight children by herself in Colored Town, in the northwest corner of Miami. Six girls and two boys. Among the girls was a child named Bessie Mae.

On this particular evening, Bessie Mae needed to hear The Word. Her siblings had asked her to look at the full moon. Normally, the moon was a welcoming sight on a sweltering night in the middle of a Miami summer. The homes in Colored Town were small, stuffy, and often dark. A moonlit night lifted everyone's spirits. Unless they were being teased by their brothers and sisters.

"See the moon?" they'd say to Bessie Mae. "See that dark spot on the moon? That's a man who was working on a Sunday, 'stead of bein' in church. The moon come down and scooped him up."

COLORED TOWN—BESSIE MAE'S OLD NEIGHBORHOOD WAS EQUAL PARTS FAITH AND STRIVING.

Marian Cooper and her husband arrived in Miami in 1919, she from Exuma, he from Cat Island. They represented the tail end of a mass migration of Bahamians to the mainland. Pushed by a faltering island economy and the lure of agricultural and construction work, islanders flocked by the tens of thousands on ferries to Miami.

As Bessie Mae put it many years later, "I learned God will provide you with everything you need."

By 1920, Bahamians made up 52 percent of the city's black community. Some settled in Coconut Grove, south of downtown, to work the lush local fields. Others gravitated north, helping with the construction of Henry Flagler's railroad and the multitude of buildings being erected in Miami's downtown.

Bahamians adapted quickly. They were experts at quarrying the local limestone, having done similar work back home. Women were prized as cooks, laundresses, seamstresses, and housekeepers. Marian Cooper was a housekeeper. To understand how she raised eight children on a domestic's wages, even managing to send one child to college, in an era when blacks were less than second-class citizens, is to understand how Bessie Mae made a success of herself, and passed those success lessons on to the grandson she raised, Chad Johnson. It's a story that is equal parts faith and striving. Marian raised Bessie never to allow her life to be defined by others. That was quite a lesson in Miami in the first half of the 20th century. The city was as racially divided as any in the country.

There is a lot of Bessie Mae in Chad. As he says, "I am who I am because of my grandmother." Let's return, then, to the Miami of Bessie's birth.

Almost as soon as blacks from the Bahamas and the mainland South began arriving en masse in Miami, during the last two decades of the late 19th century, restrictive clauses appeared in land deeds, assuring that blacks would be excluded from owning land. The only exception was a portion of the city, mostly wild and overgrown, northwest of downtown. This was where white Miami determined its black population would live. The area became known as Colored Town, or Nigger Town. By 1960, the name had changed again, to Overtown. Overtown became synonymous with poverty, racial tension and riots.

In 1919, when Marian Cooper arrived, Colored Town was a thriving, if poor, community. The population boomed, but the restrictive land deeds already made overcrowding a problem. A lack of basic services made things worse. Few streets were paved, few homes had indoor plumbing or electricity. Most of the houses in Colored Town were flimsy and wood-framed. It was "a squalid, congested district of unpaved streets lined with rickety houses and shacks," wrote Marvin Dunn, in his 1997 book, *Black Miami in the Twentieth Century*.

A lack of sanitation caused flu and yellow fever epidemics in Colored Town, and occasional outbreaks of smallpox. Infant mortality there was twice what it was in white Miami, yet Colored Town didn't have its own hospital until 1918.

This was the environment into which Bessie Mae Cooper was born. Marian Cooper was strict with all her children, rarely letting them out of her sight. "She would not let us out, not in that element," Bessie Mae recalls. "It was in the worst section of Overtown." The kids could play outdoors, but had to be home before dark.

"See that sun going down? That means you better be in the house," Marian Cooper would say. Cooper wasn't interested in hearing much feedback from her children, either. "Stop squawking like a hen!" she'd say, when the chatter became excessive.

Bessie Mae couldn't date until she was 18. She could go to the movies, if she took her nephew. She was allowed, at age 11, to join the Girl Scouts. She doesn't recall ever wanting for anything. "We were never hungry, or envious of what anyone else had," she remembered years later.

"We couldn't afford a loaf of bread. But every Friday night, my mother would mix up a bowl of dough and sit it on the shelf to rise. It would be enough for five loaves of bread. She'd say, 'This bread is for the whole week.' We'd eat it in two days.

"She'd cook a big pot of lima bean soup, with white rice. She'd get just a little bit of sausage, and cut it up into tiny pieces, and put the whole thing in a tomato gravy."

Marian worked six days a week. Unlike some of her neighbors, she came home each night, to cook and do laundry. Those housekeepers who worked "on premises" at a white family's home made more money, but spent the week away from their children. Bessie Mae recalls that was not an issue in Colored Town. It was a tight-knit community, where people looked after one another:

"Your mother could go to work on premises. Stay all week, be home Sunday. She could leave behind a house full of children, and it'd be OK. Your neighbor would watch the children."

Years later, when the local and federal governments decided to extend Interstate 95, directly through the heart of what had been renamed Overtown, families were dislodged and local businesses destroyed. The sense of community that had distinguished Colored Town would be fractured forever, leaving in its wake anger, resentment, and racial unease.

Not that Colored Town was free of that when Bessie Mae Cooper was growing up. Overcrowding encouraged by the

The Liberty Square housing project opened in the late 1930s, the first public housing project for blacks in the South. Whites wanted the blacks to stay in Colored Town.

restrictive land laws made for a tense situation almost immediately. The Liberty Square housing project would ease somewhat the congestion, and the tension. But Liberty Square would not happen until the late 1930s. In the meantime, the struggle continued between blacks who needed more space and whites who wanted them confined to Colored Town. Bahamian blacks in Miami were better educated than their mainland counterparts. Their clergymen were more vocal about the need for greater racial equality. White Miami viewed them as troublemakers. Conflict ensued.

For years an underground presence, the Ku Klux Klan announced itself officially in Miami in the summer of 1921, with a massive downtown parade. By 1925, the local klavern counted 1,500 members.

In 1921, the Klan kidnapped a white preacher named Phillip Irwin, who pastored for a black church. Irwin was "beaten, tarred, feathered, ordered to leave Miami within forty-eight hours," according to an article in the *Florida Historical Quarterly* by Miami historian Paul George. The Klan marked the occasion by building an obelisk at the county courthouse, where they'd dumped Irwin on the lawn. The monument bore this inscription: "On this Spot a few years ago a white man was found who had been tarred and feathered because he Preached Social Equality to Negroes."

Religion was the cornerstone to life in Colored Town. No one was more fervent than Marian Cooper. Church wasn't just a part of life for her and her children. It was a way of life. As Bessie Mae put it many years later, "I learned God will provide you with everything you need." (Bessie says she tried to raise her daughter, Paula Johnson, and her grandson Chad the same way. She claims she wasn't successful. A listen to Chad's cell phone message now suggests otherwise: "God first," it begins.)

One writer in the 1930s referred to Colored Town as "a city of churches." Sunday was all-day church for the Coopers: Sunday school, regular services, night church, the Baptist Young People's Union.

"Every child was there," Bessie Mae recalls. "St. Agnes, St. Francis, St. Matthew, Bethel, Mt. Zion," she said, ticking off names of churches. "We always knew where everybody was."

Nor was life in Colored Town entirely unpleasant the other six days of the week. Far from it.

An ironic benefit of strict segregation was, it caused black-owned businesses and entertainment venues within the

Bessie's mother arrived in Colored Town in 1919, when it was thriving but incredibly poor.
"A squalid, congested district of unpaved streets," wrote one historian.

community to flourish. In his book, Marvin Dunn describes an area of thriving business and entertainment. Avenue G, Colored Town's commercial heart, contained grocery stores, hardwares, a pharmacy, an ice cream parlor, a newspaper and rooming houses. A soft drink bottling plant and a hotel would follow.

Avenue G was renamed Second Avenue in the 1920s. The stretch between Sixth and Tenth Avenues became so renowned for its theatres and nightclubs, it was dubbed "Little Broadway" and "the Great Black Way." Between 1930 and 1960, every famous black entertainer played the clubs along Second Avenue.

On any given night, Count Basie could be conducting at the Harlem Square Club while Billie Holiday was astounding people with her voice at the Cotton Club a few blocks away. Ella Fitzgerald was a frequent visitor. So were Louis Armstrong, Nat King Cole, B.B. King, Sammy Davis Jr. and, later, Sam and Dave, James Brown, and Aretha Franklin.

Fun of a different sort could be had in Hardieville, a Colored Town precinct named for Miami sheriff Dan Hardie. Hardie rid white North Miami of prostitution by sending all the ladies of the evening to Hardieville. Their clientele remained largely white.

On Saturday nights, Second Avenue was jammed with traffic. Blacks might not have been allowed in white establishments; the whites had no problem frequenting the black-owned places in Colored Town.

Yet there was always something for Miami's blacks to deal with. If it weren't discrimination or white terrorism, courtesy of the KKK, it was nature: Oppressive heat, sickness and, of course, hurricanes.

In 1926, nobody knew much about hurricanes but their destructive power. Certainly, no one could predict them with any degree of accuracy. Knowledge was so limited that the notion of a hurricane's "eye" was foreign to many. That September, a powerful hurricane struck Miami. The leading edge of the storm didn't do much of the damage; the trailing edge, the portion behind the eye, did the city in.

Winds reached 138 miles an hour. "The wind was blowing so hard that it picked up our house and moved it to another location . . . while we were still inside," recalled a Colored Town resident named Calvin Johnson, in *Black Miami in the Twentieth Century*.

After the initial storm, Miamians assumed the worst was over.

Some even ventured out to the just-completed Venetian Causeway, linking downtown with Miami Beach, to assess the damage while standing in bright sunshine and under blue skies. Thirty minutes later, the storm's back side emerged with a fury. Many on the causeway died, trapped by rising waters and brutal winds.

Ultimately, 392 Miamians perished in the storm, 6,281 were hurt. Department stores were used as shelters; the streets stank from the smell of rotting fish and drying mud. Nearly 18,000 families were left homeless. Colored Town, owing to the flimsy nature of its housing stock, was hit especially hard.

Bessie Mae Cooper's house survived. Every year during hurricane season, Marian had a plan for her children. When the wind picked up, she would pack each of her children a bag full of food, and set it on the front stoop. The kids were to pick up their bags and go to Booker T. Washington High School, where a shelter had been set up, and ride out the storm. Marian Cooper would stay with her house and hope the wind wouldn't blow it away.

Years later, Bessie Mae recalled that those moments were always frightening, teary-eyed affairs. She remembered, too, that none of the children ever left their mother for the relative safety of Booker T. High.

After graduating from Booker T. Washington, Bessie Mae celebrated by spending the summer in New York. She returned to find her sister, packing a trunk.

"Are you going somewhere?" she asked her sister.

"No," the sister answered, "but you are."

Marian had arranged it. Through her church pastor, she'd gotten Bessie a free ride to Morris College, a Baptist-affiliated school in Sumter, South Carolina. The family's pastor had been the college roommate of the Morris president. Morris agreed to take Bessie on a work scholarship. The day after she came home from New York, Marian put her on a train.

Bessie recalled recently that her "job" at Morris College consisted of ringing a bell in the women's dormitory, signifying that visiting hours for the men were over.

Bessie didn't want to go away to college. "I was depressed," she said years later. She spent two years at Morris. After her second year, Marian told her she didn't have the money to pay for Bessie's bus ride home. After crying all night, Bessie borrowed the money and vowed she'd never leave Florida again.

"I'll make you a deal," she said to her mother. "I'll go back to college, if I can go to school in Florida." Marian Cooper relented. Her daughter enrolled at Bethune-Cookman, in Daytona Beach. She graduated in 1957, with a degree in elementary education.

Bessie Mae returned to a different Miami. In about 1960, Colored Town had changed its name to Overtown, partly to eliminate the use of what had become a pejorative term. Marvin Dunn, the Miami historian and a professor at Florida International University, wrote that the change also occurred because the blacks living in Coconut Grove south of downtown had to go "over town" to get to the shopping and entertainment areas of Colored Town.

Overtown had the same problems and virtues as Colored Town had, historically. Blacks were no longer restricted in their choice of places to live—at least not legally—and many had begun to migrate several miles north, to Liberty City, where they had gardens and small yards and at least a suggestion of safety. The trickle became a flood in the mid-'60s.

The coming of desegregation also hurt Overtown. Now that blacks were able to shop elsewhere, the appeal of their own stores and clubs was diminished. Then came the decision to route

Interstate 95 through the community. "They just parked it right through there," said Miami historian Paul George. The people of Overtown objected, but nobody listened. "There was no citizen empowerment," George explained, years later. "If they'd tried to run it through a rich neighborhood, it could have been stopped."

As it was, the freeway tore the community apart. As historian Marvin Dunn wrote, "The interstate ripped through the center of Overtown, wiping out massive amounts of housing as well as Overtown's main business district—the business and cultural heart of black Miami."

Before the I-95 intrusion, 40,000 people called Overtown home. Afterward, fewer than 10,000 remained. Bessie Mae and her young daughter Paula had left the community before the interstate was complete. She had seen the area begin to decline, and she wanted a yard for her daughter.

Yet she still rues what happened to her once-vibrant neighborhood. "I-95 destroyed the community. They tore down the houses and tore down the stores. Now they're talking about putting another on-off ramp through there. If they do that, there won't be anything left," she said. "People will protest. We protested before. It won't do any good."

Riots opened and closed the decade of the '80s in Overtown, both provoked by the killings of black men by Miami police officers. What hurricanes and a highway couldn't destroy, the riots did. People who'd felt disenfranchised from the beginning felt even more helpless in 1980, after an all-white jury across the state in Tampa acquitted the white cops who bludgeoned to death a black man named Arthur McDuffie, after a traffic stop.

Wrote Marvin Dunn, "It represented the truest, most damning test of the entire legal system (that blacks) had been counseled was their best hope for achieving equal treatment in American society." By 1980, the routine unrest in Overtown had spread to Liberty City, home of Bessie Mae Flowers and her grandson, Chad Johnson. Police were saying of Liberty City's mean streets, "Rocks and bottles on Saturday night are more or less a common thing here."

Chad Johnson had been 11 years old exactly a week on January 16, 1989, when a Miami police officer shot a black motorcyclist, killing the driver and his passenger, another black man. The riot that began in Overtown spread, as if by habit, to Liberty City. Miami was on center stage that week: It was six days before the Cincinnati Bengals would play the San Francisco 49ers at Joe Robbie Stadium in Ft. Lauderdale, in the Super Bowl.

One person died in the riot. Damages were estimated at $1 million. Smoke from the fires set by rioters in Overtown and Liberty City could be seen from the balconies of posh hotel rooms in downtown Miami.

Ten months later, a jury found Miami policeman William Lozano guilty of manslaughter and sentenced him to seven years in prison. Lawyers claimed a win for the legal system and declared the end of rioting in black Miami. Too late, it seems, for Bessie Mae Flowers' Overtown.

She still goes to church there, at Mt. Olivette Baptist. Instead of the throngs of parishioners she once saw, all decked out in their Sunday best, she sees clots of loitering youth, hindering her way into the sanctuary. "They hang on the corner and ask for money," she said. "They don't ask for a quarter anymore. Now, it's a dollar. I tell them, 'You want a dollar? Here's an application for a job.'"

Marian Cooper died when Bessie Mae was 25. The house the family lived in, once located at 349 NW 13th Street, is gone. The location is an underpass for Interstate 95.

Bessie Mae Flowers recalls what her mother had said, and takes strength in it, still: *Oh ye of little faith, why art thou so fearful?*

She moved from Overtown in 1964, to the house in Liberty City where she is now retired. She has seen some things. She protected her daughter and her grandson from seeing much of it.

The same way her mother protected her.

THE WAY OUT

Way out

$\mathcal{F}$ootball in Florida isn't like football anywhere else, and football in south Florida isn't like football anywhere else in the state. In the poorer black sections of Miami and surrounding Dade and Broward counties, football is a religion and a culture. It is pride and passion and the ultimate Way Out.

The University of Miami Hurricanes didn't start winning lots of football games until a white coach named Howard Schnellenberger took over the program in 1979, and began cruising the streets of Liberty City in a white Lincoln Town Car. Schnellenberger would roll up to street corners, ease down the Lincoln's tinted windows, and pass out Hurricanes' T-shirts to the kids.

Schnellenberger wasn't the first coach to realize how good the youth and high school football was in Miami. He was the first to

44

Miami Lakes Optimist
Football
1987

ETERNAL OPTIMISTS—CHAD'S FIRST POSITION WAS NOSE TACKLE.

maximize its potential. His Hurricanes won their first national championship in 1983, with a team full of local players.

Miami would win four national college titles in nine years, and five between '83 and 2001. When the 'Canes weren't winning it all, Florida State was, in 1993 and 1999. One or both schools contend for the championship every year, along with the University of Florida. Each does it with a large helping of home cooking.

Says Dennis Erickson, now the coach at Idaho, who coached the Hurricanes to national titles in 1989 and 1991, "You could come awfully close to winning a national championship with kids just from Dade and Broward counties."

Given the traditions that have been developed at the three schools, and the reputations they've earned for getting their players into the National Football League, it is hard to get a Florida high school player to leave Florida.

That doesn't stop every big-time college football program in the country from trying. Says Boston College coach Tom O'Brien, "You can try to get them out of there, but mostly you'll hear they want to be a Hurricane, a Seminole, or a Gator. It's usually, 'You can recruit him, but he's going to Miami.' That's what they see on TV growing up. Those are the players they see coming back to the neighborhood."

"Football is so big here, high school coaches come watch the little kids."

O'Brien was an assistant at the University of Virginia in 1983. The Cavaliers' football program had been a joke forever, partly because they'd been unable to recruit elite black athletes. "White

meat" was the derogatory term applied to UVA football
by a former Clemson coach, Frank Howard.

O'Brien arrived at Virginia from Navy, with head coach
George Welsh. Welsh's first directive to his assistant was, "Get me
some guys who can run."

O'Brien knew what that meant. He headed for Florida.
Specifically, the southern end of the state.

It wasn't a revelation in college football in the 1980s that teams
with fast players had a decided edge over teams without as much
speed. It took Miami's stunning success to ram the point home.
Schools such as Ohio State, Penn State, Nebraska, and Oklahoma,
which traditionally had relied on size and strength, were being
outflanked by the Florida schools. The need for speed quickly
became apparent to any team interested in winning.

Tom O'Brien found a kid named John Ford. Ford was from
Belle Glade, an agricultural town some ninety minutes west of
Palm Beach, on the southern shore of Lake Okeechobee. Ford was
a wide receiver on his high school football team and a sprinter on
the track team. He honed his speed by chasing rabbits in the sugar
cane fields. Once the cane was burned off after the harvest, the
fields were open, and the rabbits had nowhere to hide. Ford and
his friends amused themselves by running the creatures down and
catching them.

Unlike most of his peers, Ford wanted to leave the state.
He signed with Virginia and immediately was what coaches call a
"difference maker." Ford's freshman year, the Cavaliers went to the
Peach Bowl, their first bowl invitation ever.

Imagine a team of John Fords.

Picture a roster full of players with speed, even the linemen.
Think how good they'd be if all their natural gifts had been
nurtured since the age of 4. That's what happens in places like

Liberty City. When Chad Johnson was 4, he played football in full pads. He was a nose tackle.

Narrow your eyes a little more, and picture all this taken to an extreme: Local high school coaches scouting teams of 75-pound players. Coaches who transport their 95-pound teams to and from games in Hummer limousines, coaches who award their players gold rings for winning a Pop Warner Super Bowl title, the national championship contested every year in Orlando, where kid-players as light as 65 pounds spend several nights in Disney-owned hotel rooms.

Imagine, too, local gang members scouting practices, so they know which Pop Warner team to bet on, on Saturday afternoon. And parents threatening coaches with physical violence, when their children's teams don't meet inevitably high (and not always realistic) expectations.

Take in all that, and you will have Optimist League football in Miami. Chad Johnson didn't get his competitiveness waiting for the school bus to Beach High. He was all but born with it. Though he played just one season with the Liberty City Optimists, as an eighth-grader, Johnson was immersed in the culture of football from the time he could pull on a helmet.

In Liberty City, Optimist football started with a do-gooder named Sam Johnson and a musician named Luther Campbell. The unlikely pair, one a dreamer, the other a realist and Liberty City philanthropist, started in 1990 a program that has nurtured the aspirations of thousands of kids, and their parents.

When Sam Johnson and Campbell grew up in Liberty City, there were no organized sports for the kids. You went to the park to play pick-up games or, if you were Campbell, you hopped a bus nine miles, to Miami Beach, where there were leagues.

By the time Sam Johnson got to high school, he didn't have

much time for sports. The oldest of five children, living with their single mother, Johnson worked after school. He lied about his age, taking various jobs, "Anything that would pay a dollar," he says now.

He promised himself then that a lack of money would never keep any of his children from playing sports. Little did he know his pledge would be expanded to cover an entire neighborhood's children for the last sixteen years, and counting.

Sam Johnson met Luther Campbell when he asked the musician to sponsor an awards banquet for the kids' baseball teams in Liberty City. Baseball was Sam Johnson's first love. He became executive director of the Liberty City Optimists initially to oversee the baseball operation. Johnson had twelve kids in the program.

"I was just trying to give back to the community," he says. "I wasn't looking for it to blow up." Johnson drove a metro bus for a living. He organized his work schedule so he could run the program when the kids got out of school. His bus routes began at 3:55 a.m. and ran until 4 in the afternoon.

When Johnson approached Campbell about sponsoring the awards banquet, Campbell had a better idea. "Hey, man," he said. "Let's do football."

In 1990, Luther Campbell and his group 2 Live Crew were becoming famous. Or notorious, depending on your perspective. The group's debut album, *As Nasty As They Wanna Be*, which included a single called "Me So Horny," had been deemed obscene by a Broward County judge, who counted eighty-seven references to oral sex on the album. The court fight went all the way to the Supreme Court, which ruled in Campbell's favor.

Fortified by a legal victory and all the attendant and deliciously good publicity, *As Nasty As They Wanna Be* went double platinum, two million copies sold. Luther Campbell of Liberty City was suddenly wealthy, and wanting to give back to his neighborhood. Football was a natural.

As Campbell put it, in Robert Andrew Powell's 2003 book, *We Own This Game*, "In Miami, you got to play football in order to even have any kind of man in you. It's almost like football is like becoming a man. It's a whole part of showing that you are tough. And in Miami, it's mostly blacks that play the game."

Football kept kids off the mean streets and gave them a purpose and goals beyond hanging out on the corner. Football has become a source of community pride in Liberty City where, in the years since the Optimist program was launched, the youth football has been overwhelmingly good. The hope it offers is tangible, in a place where hope can be in short supply.

As one Liberty City Optimist football coach said in Powell's book, "Take Pop Warner ball. That's what gets you into high school, which is what gets you into college, which is from where you make the pros. They know that if they do go to college and make it to the NFL, they gonna get the big payday."

Success doesn't come free. Youth football in Miami has had its share of real-life intrusions. In the 1990s, local drug gangs known as the Boobie Boys and the John Does infected Liberty City. Their influence filtered down to the football programs. Their members occasionally were spotted by coaches "scouting" football practices, seeking insight to be used while gambling.

As Powell writes, "It was nothing for a Boobie Boy or a John Doe to drop a $10,000 bet on his favorite team. And not only at the high school level, but in Pop Warner as well."

So-called "street agents" took care of players, often long before they got to college, hoping in some cases to broker (for a fee) the player's services to a college. Or, later on, to hook up the player with an agent, who would represent him during contract talks with NFL teams.

The best players were always looked after. Chad Johnson's friend and mentor, Terrence "T-Dog" Craig, a lifelong Liberty City resident, said the area's drug dealers steered clear of players they believed had a chance of "making it out" of Liberty City. Johnson was among that group.

Regardless, the phenomenal success and growth of the youth football program is indisputable. With Campbell's seed money, Sam Johnson chartered the Liberty City Optimists football program, in October 1990. Now, there are eleven teams of Warriors playing Pop Warner football, in nine divisions, from 65 pounds to 145. The program has 130 coaches, all volunteer, for football and cheerleading. Even with eleven teams, kids are cut.

"The maximum is thirty-five per team," Johnson explained. "We get between 500 and 600 kids coming out."

Most start by the time they reach first or second grade. "They're raised up in the program," Johnson said. There are so many teams now, Johnson has had to start scheduling two games on Friday nights, in addition to the standard all-day Saturday contests. As many as 5,000 people attend.

Not far from the Liberty City Optimist Club's office in Hadley Park, on the southern edge of Liberty City, the Gwen Cherry Boys and Girls Club stands like a hope beacon among boarded-up housing projects. In their first season, the Liberty City Warriors won city titles in seven of eight weight divisions. That success created an enthusiasm in the local community that led to programs being founded at several other local parks, Gwen Cherry among them.

It continues to this day. Last fall, when the Warriors won the 130-pound Pop Warner national title, their biggest competition came from the Gwen Cherry 130s, coached by Luther Campbell.

The first time the NFL brought the Super Bowl back to Miami after the 1989 riots was in 1995. The league donated $1 million then, for a recreation facility at Gwen Cherry Park. The NFL Youth Education Town features a full-sized gym, two football fields and two computer labs.

"The kids have to come in here and do their homework first, before they can play sports," said Tyrone Hilton, the assistant unit director for the Gwen Cherry Boys and Girls Club. He can speak to the influence football has on lives in Liberty City.

"Coaches fill needs in life beyond sports," Hilton says. "It's always been that way here. Kids will think, 'My father is not in my life, but my mom is, and my coaches are.'"

Hilton's small office, just off the front hallway of the clean, well-maintained club, is crammed with trophies. Gwen Cherry has won a national Pop Warner title, and is a prime feeder club for Northwestern High School, legendary in Florida for supplying players to colleges and the NFL.

"Football is so big here, high school coaches come watch the little kids," said Hilton, "the way the college coaches watch the high school kids most other places."

It all takes money. The Warriors' home field has a digital irrigation system, "just like a pro or college team," Sam Johnson said. Uniforms might not be new, but they're in good condition. Johnson has every helmet reconditioned every year, at a cost of several thousand dollars.

Warriors teams have been to the Pop Warner Super Bowl several times. That requires transportation and several nights of lodging at Disney World in Orlando, none of which is paid for. Johnson calls himself "a professional beggar," constantly hitting up local governments for money. The NFL has donated money. Nike

paid for a scoreboard. What Sam Johnson really wants is
for those who have benefited from his program not to forget it.

"Somebody sacrificed their life for this to happen," Johnson
said. "You have to make it, then come back."

Chad Johnson never strayed. His grandmother, Bessie Mae
Flowers, might have taken him out of the neighborhood, for school
and sports. She might have insisted that while he might have lived
in Liberty City, he wasn't of it. Chad himself might have sought
his fortunes in colleges on the West Coast, then found them in
the Midwest, as a professional in Cincinnati. But he never really
left Liberty City. His favorite expression is, "You can't know where
you're going until you understand where you've been."

Every off-season, Chad Johnson returns to Liberty City, to live
in the house where he grew up. Even as he is having a large house
of his own built in Davie, an hour up I-95, Johnson will gravitate
back to Liberty City, out of pride, memory, appreciation and need.
It's his security blanket, to be worn as protection from the fallout
of fame. Those who know him best knew him first.

The all-night glitz of the Miami Beach club scene is ten
miles south. The Bahamas are a short boat ride away. Miami is
an eclectic, electric city, vibrant with ethnic diversity, alive with
possibility. People with lots of money and lots of free time can do
what they want in Miami, and be whom they please. More often
than not, Chad Johnson can be found at his grandmother's house,
watching ESPN on TV.

When he's home, Johnson runs on the track at Northwestern
High, early in the morning. Last fall, during the Bengals bye week,
he returned to Gwen Cherry Park, to preside over a whole day
of Pop Warner football games that became known as the Chad
Johnson Bowl. He announced, "I want to be the water boy," a
position he held as a kid at Northwestern High games.

He helped pay for Gwen Cherry's new scoreboard, he makes sure the players get new football shoes. He has been known to attend games and peel off $100 bills for kids who make especially good plays. Two years ago, before the Bengals played the Denver Broncos on Monday Night Football, Johnson called Ty Hilton at the boys and girls club.

"Make sure you tell the kids to watch," he told Hilton. "I'm gonna do Champ Bailey in." Bailey was Denver's Pro Bowl defensive back. Johnson starred in Cincinnati's 23-10 upset victory, catching seven passes for 149 yards, including a 50-yard touchdown pass in the first quarter that set the mood. The TD grab came at the expense of Champ Bailey.

Chad Johnson remains a hopeful presence in a community that needs one. "The areas these guys come up in, the odds are long," Ty Hilton is saying. "When you see guys come back like Chad and Willis McGahee (a former University of Miami star by way of nearby Central High School, now a running back for the Buffalo Bills), it makes a difference."

Football was Chad Johnson's way up and way out. Liberty City youth football, in all its glory and imperfection, sent him on his way. He isn't likely to forget.

Beach
LIFE'S A BEACH

It was fated that Chad Johnson would end up at Miami Beach High School, alma mater of actors Mickey Rourke and Andy Garcia and former ESPN personality Roy Firestone, ten blocks from the high-life glamor of South Beach. What better place for a would-be performer than a stage abutting one of the country's ritziest entertainment strips? Not to mention that Beach High was three blocks from Nautilus Middle School, where Bessie Mae Flowers taught. Keeping her thumb on her hyperactive, mischievous grandson was about as easy as flexing her hand.

"Miz Rolle and I used to compare pink slips," Flowers recalled recently. Samari Rolle's mother also worked at Nautilus. Her son attended Beach with Chad. They're cousins. Neither Samari nor Chad was terribly attuned to school. The pink slips were phone messages, taken by the secretary at Nautilus, while Flowers and Rolle were in the classroom. The people at Beach phoned frequently, regarding their boys.

THE GRADUATE—HALLELUJAH!

Both boys made it through Beach. Samari Rolle played college football at Florida State, on a football scholarship; Chad Johnson's grades wouldn't allow that. He took a longer road. Each became a star in the National Football League, but not before prompting many pink slips in high school, though Flowers acknowledges she took first place in that competition.

Throughout its eighty-two-year history, Miami Beach High School has been acutely reflective of the racial and social evolution of Miami and Dade County. As late as the early 1960s, Beach High was the province of upper-middle-class Jewish kids who were well-mannered, needed little discipline, and went on to college. In the forty years hence, the school's population has become overwhelmingly Hispanic, as droves of Cubans and Latinos flocked to south Florida in search of a better life.

"You can't tell me this person or that person isn't a good person, simply because of skin color."

The area has evolved constantly and rapidly. By 1985, according to Marvin Dunn's book *Black Miami in the Twentieth Century*, 23,000 children were being bused to schools outside their home districts, in what would prove an ultimately unsuccessful attempt to desegregate Miami-area schools. Fifteen years before that, the area had adopted a "majority to minority" transfer program. Children could transfer from a school where their race was a majority, to one where they were in the minority.

Many more African-American kids transferred from their local schools to majority white schools. According to Marvin Dunn, ninety-six percent of the transfer students were black. It led to overcrowding in the majority white schools. By 1985, the rule was further complicated, to state that black children could not transfer to mostly white schools that were at least fifteen percent over capacity. Once the number of black students reached thirty-seven percent, transfers would no longer be allowed.

Years later, rules changed again, majority-minority transfers were discouraged and children attended schools within their districts.

Into this confusing landscape landed Chad Johnson, who could have gone to Beach High, regardless. His grandmother taught in the district. Chad's enrollment was assured. At least a decade before Chad arrived, Beach High was a palatable human stew of racial and ethnic backgrounds. It was majority Hispanic, but with a considerable black and white population. Everyone got along. Says Rick DiVita, the current head football coach at Beach, and a teacher and coach there since 1987, "We had all different races and religions. It was very diverse then, and I thought very good for the kids. It opened your eyes to the world we live in. Our debate teams were as good as our athletic teams."

Johnson would have a similar experience in three years at Santa Monica College, a two-year school in the Los Angeles suburbs. Santa Monica was as diverse as the sprawling metropolis from which it drew its students. For students accustomed to living in areas where nearly everyone was of the same race and ethnicity, SMC was an eye opener. As Eugene Sykes, an SMC teammate of Johnson's, explained, "Santa Monica is a bunch of commuters. All kinds of cultures. Pretty much every culture. For African-Americans from South Central (a predominantly black L.A. neighborhood), it was a great place to be.

"It was like, 'You can't tell me this person or that person isn't a good person, simply because of skin color.' I know they're better than that. I've been to school with these people."

Johnson had that sort of experience his entire life. His grandmother had purposely sent Johnson out of their mostly black neighborhood of Liberty City, to schools that were either largely white or racially mixed. That might explain why Johnson is so comfortable with all kinds of people today.

He certainly had no problem mingling with the other 2,200 students at Beach. Johnson didn't clown his way through high school to find his niche among his racially diverse classmates. He clowned his way through because that was who he was. Says Dale Sims, an assistant football coach at Beach for nineteen years, "I just remember him running around, having people chase him. A lot of the time you didn't take him seriously. His thing was to have fun. It wasn't just general clowning. It was pretty specific clowning, all involving him." The exception came on the football field.

He played wide receiver his first three years at Beach. "Caught everything you threw to him," says Rick DiVita. The head coach, Jim Kroll, shifted Johnson to quarterback his senior year. "We took the best athlete we had and put him at quarterback," Kroll explains now. It was a philosophy started a few years earlier, with Duane Starks and Rolle. Both would go on to star in the NFL, as defensive backs.

Jim Kroll says Johnson was a "good high school quarterback," but not in the same league with Starks and Rolle. That would be the assessment of all his coaches at Beach. Unlike Starks and Rolle and another Beach standout, Terry Cousin, Johnson was not seen as a major college prospect. His skills were good, not great, and his grades were always suspect. Plus, as Sims puts it, "You didn't think he'd be serious enough long enough for anyone to give him the time of day."

The coaches were accurate in that assessment. It took Johnson one abbreviated stop at an Oklahoma junior college and three years at Santa Monica before he finally made it as a Division I player, at Oregon State. "Samari and Duane jumped out at you," Kroll says. "I was thinking Chad would go to college and get a job."

Johnson did show flashes of what was to come. Sims tells the story of the day after practice when Johnson beat him on a deep pass pattern. Sims calls it "getting bombed." He swears that, even today at age 51, no Beach player before or since had ever bombed him but Chad Johnson.

Sims was a track star at Southern University who at age 40 could still cover 40 yards in 4.3 seconds, world class speed. The wide receivers and special teams coach at Beach, Sims enjoyed challenging his players to post-practice pass-catching sessions. He and his players would each take a turn playing wideout and defensive back. The idea was to run straight fly patterns and have the backup quarterback throw bombs. Best man wins.

"It was just one of those things we did after practice. One-on-one, in-your-face bump and run," Sims recalls. The backup quarterback Johnson's senior year was never able to grasp the offense completely enough to run it, but he could throw the ball 65 yards. Chad lined up at wideout. Sims was up in his face. Each took off running as fast as he could.

The way Sims recalls it now, the pass was overthrown, uncatchable. He eased off the play, not wanting to risk injury, to himself or Johnson. "The ball was five or six yards out of his reach," says Sims. "He dove and caught it on his fingertips. He ended up on his back."

Johnson bounced up, laughing hysterically. "You got bombed! I bombed you!" he screamed to Sims.

"I'll be damned," was all Sims said about that.

"I knew he was fast, but after that I went and told Kroll, 'This kid is special.' No way he catches that ball. Chad could have been a state track champion in the 400 meters. We'll never know for sure, because he never came out. He was too busy clowning around."

A few years later, Sims would see a repeat of that same catch, entirely by accident. After Johnson left Beach, he spent less than a semester at Langston University in Oklahoma in 1996. After that, his high school coaches lost track of him. Until one day in 2000. Sims was at home one Saturday when his phone rang. It was Rick DiVita. "You wouldn't believe who's playing for Oregon State," DiVita said to Sims.

Another Beach assistant coach was watching the game on satellite TV. When he heard the name Chad Johnson mentioned on the broadcast, he dialed up DiVita, who then called Sims.

"I was totally amazed," says Sims today. "Then I saw him run a curl route. He curled inside, the ball was thrown to the outside. He caught it falling backwards, on his fingertips. He was out there, lying on his back. It was déjà vu."

Another Beach High assistant coach became an important part of Johnson's life at the time. Terrence Craig, known universally as "T-Dog," coached the team's offensive line. Craig attended Texas Southern University, where he played with future NFL star Michael Strahan. He met Chad Johnson in 1992, when Johnson was a high school freshman.

"A snot-nosed kid," Craig called him.

Craig grew up in Liberty City and was wise to its pitfalls. Like Johnson, he was raised in a father-less household, and understood that success in that environment required male guidance. "I was like a daddy figure for Chad. I kept his behind out of trouble. I know about the dope dealers and the robbers. I told him, they go left, you go right. I kept him from the wrong crowd," Craig said.

Johnson's grandfather, James Flowers, did his best to keep his grandson on the up and up as well. "I'll break your legs if you cross 12ᵗʰ Avenue," Johnson recalls James telling him, 12ᵗʰ Avenue being, in James' mind, a line of demarcation between acceptable acquaintances and thugs. James was a persistent presence in Chad's life. He could be found behind the bench at his grandson's youth football games, offering coaches unsolicited advice. "Coach, let him rest," James might say. "His legs are tired."

James Flowers was murdered when Johnson was at Beach High. He had separated from Bessie by then. He was at a party when the shots rang out. "The lady of the house said all she heard James say was, 'No, man, no,'" Bessie recalled, years later. "She opened the door, Jimmy fell in. They never found out who did it. I don't think they tried to find out."

"Mommy, why did they have to shoot him?" Chad asked Bessie Mae not long after James died.

"I don't know, Chad," she said. "There are bad people in this world. I can't tell you, 'Don't feel bad.' It was his time. The Lord giveth. The Lord taketh."

T-Dog would give Chad a ride home from school. He'd keep the drug dealers away from him. "I protected him. He was the type of kid who had to be put in something structured to keep him out of trouble."

Craig left Beach High several years ago, to coach the offensive line at Killian High. The married father of three small children, Craig remains ten credits short of his degree in criminal justice. He also owns three state high school football title rings. "My success shows on my hands," says Craig. And in helping a hyper, impressionable kid keep his nose clean.

If Chad Johnson did not have the talent of Duane Starks or his cousin Samari Rolle, he did have the sense of purpose. "He was always looking forward to practice," DiVita recalls. "You could start practice at 11 at night and end it at 3 in the morning and he'd be there." When Sims needed a punter, he handed the ball to Johnson and after "three minutes of coaching, Chad was kicking 35-yard spirals."

Johnson's desire to win—a trait that over the years has been miscast as selfishness, all the way up to the playoff game with the Pittsburgh Steelers after the '05 season—showed itself at Beach High. Says Sims, "When Chad felt he had an opportunity to help the team and you ignored him, it was like taking energy from him."

Years later, T-Dog Craig said he could tell by Johnson's body language early in the playoff game loss to Pittsburgh that his protégé had lost his concentration. "Looked just like he did in high school when things didn't go well," said Craig, the offensive line coach at Beach High during Johnson's years there.

Sims describes the look: "Head tilted back. Feet dragging. Frustrated."

The team would end every practice with "ten perfect plays." With Johnson at quarterback, the offense would run ten of its basic plays to perfection, before the players could leave. The idea, in addition to the precision the drill fostered, was to hone the team concept. No one was perfect until everyone was. Johnson was the ringmaster during the daily quest for perfection.

"He was a strange kind of leader in that sense," says Sims. "When I watch him on TV now, the announcers say he's out there yelling at people. That's not him. He was a kid with an exceptional amount of self confidence. Kids like that want to put it all on their shoulders. He wasn't agitating. He was encouraging."

In five years with the Cincinnati Bengals, Johnson has done the same thing. If he's in quarterback Carson Palmer's ear during a game, it's almost always because Johnson thinks Johnson isn't being given enough chance to put it all on his shoulders. Johnson celebrates his touchdowns, but only when the Bengals are ahead. He complains about not getting the ball enough, but only after the Bengals have lost. Now, as in high school, what moves him most is winning. If only he'd applied that to the rest of his day at Beach High.

Most high school coaches have a little Father Flanagan in them. At that level, they're rarely in it for the money and never for the fame. It's not the perks, either. As many coaches line their own fields as do not. As many dip into their own generally shallow pockets to help kids with a meal or a pair of shoes, as those who don't.

Jim Kroll coached at Beach for sixteen years, between 1980 and 1995. He won 108 games, the most by one coach in school history, and sent six players to the NFL. He coached just one losing season. That sort of success is not what he remembers as much now. At age 62 and recently retired, Kroll recalls the off-field successes, the small ways he tweaked, for the better, a life or two. He counts Chad Johnson among those tweaks, though Kroll concedes his influence on Johnson generally was confined to making sure he went to class. And that his teachers had mercy on him when he didn't.

When Kroll coached at Beach, kids were still being bused in. The majority-to-minority program was still in effect. As Kroll says, "Beach was not an African-American school when I was there, but the football team was."

Between 1980 and 1986, kids from the football player-rich areas of Overtown and Liberty City who would have attended Northwestern High were divided equally among three schools: Miami Jackson, Miami High, and Beach. "Across the water" was the expression applied to the students coming to Beach High.

"When I was at Beach, it was a very fertile ground. These kids from Overtown, football was their ticket out," says Kroll.

By 1996, students no longer went across the water. Many stayed close to home and attended Booker T. Washington, reopened in 1996 as a high school after nearly thirty years as a middle school. Without the infusion of bused-in talent, Beach High football suffered, and still does.

That wasn't an issue for Kroll for at least his first ten years there. The larger struggle was to get some of his players through school. He recalls a few in particular: Dave Thomas, who played professionally with the Dallas Cowboys and the Jacksonville Jaguars—despite leaving Beach High with a seventh-grade reading level—and Jerry Ulysses.

Jerry Ulysses, says Kroll, was a great football player who came to Beach High unable to speak in complete sentences. If Kroll saw Ulysses wincing during a game, he might ask, "What's wrong?"

"Arm," Ulysses would say. "Arm hurt. Helmet."

An opponent had injured Ulysses' arm by hitting it with his helmet. Kroll recalls the Beach librarian criticizing him for filling Ulysses' head with football dreams.

"She wanted the kid to go to vo-tech," says Kroll.

Instead, the coach helped nurse Ulysses through high school, pleading with and cajoling his teachers, telling them the kid's football acumen could end up saving his life. Ulysses made it through high school. Kroll got him into a junior college on his football ability. Jerry Ulysses, who couldn't speak in complete sentences as a high school freshman, got a degree from the University of Cincinnati. Kroll says Ulysses is now working in the police department for Dade County. "Don't squash a kid's dream," says Kroll.

Compared with Ulysses, Chad Johnson was a merit scholar. "But I tried to do the same things for Chad. I interceded more than once to get teachers to lighten up and give him a chance," Kroll says. "I had to monitor him to keep him eligible." When Johnson graduated from Beach, after attending night summer school after his senior year, Kroll told him, "They should put my name on your diploma, as much help as I've given you."

Like lots of high school teachers who also coach, Jim Kroll's path was influenced by coaches who'd helped him. Kroll grew up in suburban Chicago, the oldest of four boys living in a working-class neighborhood. He became the first person in his family to go to college, thanks in part to the encouragement he got from three high school coaches. Kroll went to Iowa State Teachers College (now the University of Northern Iowa), graduated in 1965, and started coaching high school football six years later. He moved to Miami in 1978 and took the job at Beach High in April 1980.

When he got there, the football team was a mess. "I had to go in there with a whip and a chair," he recalls. There was talent there, but little discipline. His first year, his players fought in the huddle. "They had no concept what a team was," Kroll says. He says he adopted an "us against the world" philosophy. Kroll's motto became, "Act the way you want to become, and you'll become the way you act."

"We always emphasized team and family. I always tried to encourage kids. A pat on the back is six inches higher than a kick in the ass, and goes a lot further."

Kroll stopped coaching at Beach after the '95 season. He saw the talent pool draining away from Beach. In March 1997, he took a job at Palmetto High, closer to his home.

Rick DiVita has been the Beach High head coach for seven years. He doesn't have the athletes his predecessor had. The demographic has changed substantially, again. DiVita puts the school's black population now at just over one percent. Hispanics are prevalent now: about eighty percent of the school's population.

While the number of players on the team remains between forty and forty-five, the same as when Chad Johnson played, the quality isn't there. Most of DiVita's best players play both offense and defense. "The kids on the beach now aren't coming in as football players," he says.

Meanwhile, Booker T. Washington High's football team has reached the state title game in each of the last two seasons. In a football-mad state such as Florida, that's an impressive feat. After a few tumultuous decades of bussing and fleeing, the kids from Overtown and Liberty City are staying home. Football at Miami Beach High School will never be the same.

The soccer team has flourished, though. The Latin kids grew up playing soccer. "We almost won the state last year," Rick DiVita says.

He is at once proud and wistful.

"He was always looking forward to practice," DiVita recalled. "We could start practice at 11 at night and end it at 3 in the morning and he'd be there."

*C*had Johnson got his first last chance at Santa Monica College, a two-year commuter school not far from the Pacific Ocean. The Corsairs coach, Robert Taylor, has been there twenty-two years, always resisting the urge to move on. Taylor's motto is, "Corsair football is here to save lives." And then, in walked this kid from south Florida.

Bessie had ordered her grandson to move to Los Angeles and live with Paula. "I've done all I can do for you," she told the grandson she raised, when he returned from Langston University, having been expelled for fighting. "The choices are yours. You don't want to listen to me, you'll have to go live with your mother."

Years later, Chad Johnson would recognize that parting as a decisive moment in his life. "I don't want to know how my life would have turned out if my grandmother had let me stay home," he said. "As soon as I got out there and I enrolled at Santa Monica, it was time for football season to start."

Paula Johnson had other ideas. "Now, it's about your

FABULAR—DEMETRIUS POSEY (4) and CHAD (8) in back row; STEVE SMITH (7), second row, left; ANTHONY CEPHAS (2); QUARTERBACK DYLEN SMITH (3); EUGENE SYKES (6), in front row; and (above) COACH TAYLOR.

education," she determined. Chad had no interest in education.

He knew where Santa Monica's campus was, though. He found the football practice field easy enough. He showed up for the Corsairs' first night practice, in 1997, and simply started working out with the rest of the team, running pass patterns, as if he'd been there before.

Robert Taylor looked at one of his assistants, Dave Burrell. "Who is that guy?"

"I don't know," Burrell said.

Johnson was wearing orange shorts and black socks. Taylor approached him, his head cocked in wonder and bemusement.

"Whassup, buddy?" Johnson said to Taylor.

Robert Taylor had been coaching in the Los Angeles area for more than twenty years: L.A. Southwest College, L.A. City College, John Muir High School in Pasadena. He even did a stint at North Carolina A&T. Like lots of coaches, Taylor didn't consider his work to be a job. To him, coaching was a calling.

When he was 8, Taylor's father "just disappeared out of my life," he recalled. Taylor hasn't seen his father since. He's 61 now. "As I got older, I kind of wished I hadn't known him. It might have been easier. I'm around a lot of kids that don't have male figures in their lives. I think I can be that image for them."

As fate would have it, in sauntered Chad Johnson, who at that point never knew his own father.

"What's your name?" Taylor asked the stranger wearing black socks.

"Chad Johnson."

"Where you from?"

"Miami."

Johnson's answers were clipped and defensive.

"How'd you get here?"

"My mama said it was close."

"You could tell right away he had a chip on his shoulder," Taylor recalled recently.

"Is something wrong with you, Chad Johnson from Miami?" Taylor asked.

"Nah."

"I'm the head coach and we don't wear black socks to practice here. You come back tomorrow, with white socks and a new attitude," Taylor said.

Chad left. Taylor looked at Dave Burrell. "That boy could really run," he said to Burrell. "I sure hope he comes back tomorrow."

Chad Johnson came back the next day, with new socks and a new attitude. He wasn't an A student. But he was smart enough to recognize a last chance when he saw one.

"He changed overnight," Taylor recalls.

"I've got to give up on this boy," Collins would say. "He won't do what I tell him to do."

The coaching staff knew right away they had something. Their charge was to harness it.

"He was a wild stallion," says Craig Austin, Santa Monica's offensive coordinator at the time. "Like a thoroughbred without a saddle. I took one look at those calf muscles when he walked and I knew we had something, if we could control it."

Austin was describing Johnson's raw ability. He could also have been referring to his personality. After the fight at Langston that got him expelled—and having to return to Liberty City to face Bessie, who tough-loved him out of town—Johnson wasn't trusting a lot of people.

But he knew football was his ticket, and he knew he had no option but to get it punched. He took the bus every day, from his mother's apartment in Baldwin Hills, out to Santa Monica. He set up a weight bench in her living room. He ran everywhere he didn't ride the bus. He wore white socks to practice.

He quickly became friends with the other SMC receivers: Eugene Sykes, Anthony Cephas, Demetrius Posey, and a local kid named Stevonne Smith. Stevonne would shorten his name to Steve, spend two years at Santa Monica, two at Utah, and go on to a Pro Bowl career in the National Football League.

Johnson nicknamed the group The Fab Five. It was possibly the best group of wideouts ever to play on the same junior college team. By the time they were through, two of the five would play in the NFL; one played in the Arena Football League. Their quarterback, Dylen Smith, played professionally in Canada.

They would score 40 points a game, but give up 55. The Corsairs were half a great team. The receivers were lightning out of the bottle. Johnson, with that Miami speed, fit right in. On all counts.

Normally, you don't choose to go to junior college to play football. Not if you aspire to be a pro. Junior college is either a bus stop or a dead end. You play juco because something in your life isn't quite right: Your grades aren't good, your past is checkered. Your risk, in the eyes of those who matter, outweighs your reward. As Robert Taylor put it, "Every kid who comes through junior college has a little suitcase with him." For his personal baggage.

Chad Johnson had a steamer trunk, starting with his grades and ending with his dismissal from Langston. In the middle was his innate Chad-ness. "First impressions of Chad?" Eugene Sykes asks, repeating a question. "Same clown he is now. All he does is play around."

Johnson would arrive at practice chattering. It was as if he had a key in his back and it was perpetually being turned.

"Fab Five's here," he'd yell. "Who's gonna cover us? You can't stop us. Who are you gonna double (team)?"

When Dave Burrell had heard enough, he'd make the receivers run the bleachers as punishment. To Johnson, he would say, "The Fab Five is gonna be the Fab Four if you don't shut up."

Robert Taylor called Johnson "needy. He craved attention. If you just talked to him, he'd be fine. He'd stick to you like flypaper. There wasn't a day I didn't talk to Chad about something. It could be silly or important. It could just be something like, 'Chad, you going to class?'"

Johnson's first year at Santa Monica, Taylor hired a local coach and former Canadian Football League player named Charles Collins to coach the Corsairs' wide receivers. Collins would become the guardian angel of Chad Johnson's football career. Before Collins could do that, he had to convince himself Chad Johnson was worth the bother. He'd call Bessie Mae Flowers, at home in Miami.

"I've got to give up on this boy," Collins would say. "He won't do what I tell him to do."

"Listen to me carefully," would be Bessie's response. "Don't give up on him. Just tell him you're giving up on him. Stick with him. He'll come through."

That first year, 1997, Johnson amused and amazed everyone, with his attitude and his speed. "He was what we call a junior college character," Taylor said not long ago. "He talked a lot. He said he could play quarterback. If we ever used him at quarterback, we'd run every down."

Johnson also started wearing gold caps on his front teeth, though no one at the time believed they were real.

"Fake, definitely," Dylen Smith said recently.

Johnson also sucked his thumb, a habit left over from childhood that he maintains to this day. "He'd do that all the time, usually in meetings," said Taylor. "We'd see him doing that and we'd tell him, 'Chad, get that thumb out your mouth.'"

The competition in 1997 between members of the Fab Five was serious. They rotated in and out of games. The quarterback Dylen Smith had to be something of a ringmaster. "We'd put 60 (points) on the board, watch the film, and laugh," he recalled. "Those five guys would have to be one-upping each other every week."

Unlike his receivers, Dylen Smith was quiet and thoughtful. After getting his associates degree from Santa Monica, he went to Kansas University, starting at quarterback for the Jayhawks. Smith then signed with the Saskatchewan Roughriders of the Canadian League, then promptly tore the rotator cuff on his throwing shoulder. Arm problems would dog Smith his entire pro career.

By the spring of 2006, he'd nearly completed his bachelor's degree, in hopes of becoming a juvenile probation officer.

Dylen Smith got some training handling juveniles while working with the Fab Five. The Corsairs used a four-wideout set most of the time. If picking one to throw to weren't hard enough, the offensive line was leaky, so Smith rarely had much time to make up his mind. Once he did, it was magical: "Sixty yards, off his back foot," Eugene Sykes recalled.

Smith's diplomatic skills were equally acute. The receivers who would tell him to throw to them—usually Stevonne Smith and Chad Johnson—would be passed over for players like Sykes, who was subtle in his requests.

"I might see Dylen in the hall after a class or something, during the week," Sykes said. "I'd just remind him I could catch a little bit."

Stevonne Smith wasn't quite so low-key. "Sykes, how many catches you got?" Sykes recalls Stevonne asking him, in the huddle during a game. "Eleven? What, you running for president or something?"

Said Dylen Smith, "Stevonne and Chad wanted the ball all the time. They were always open. Just ask them. They were up in my ear all game. I didn't tell them to shut up, though. If they told me to throw them the ball, I'd throw it to Eugene. If you want to shut them up, don't throw to them. I'd give any quarterback that advice."

Years later, Chad Johnson would re-learn the lesson as a Cincinnati Bengal, seeking attention from Bengals quarterback Carson Palmer.

"One game, we're playing Moorpark College, we're getting blown out. I wasn't playing that well," said Dylen Smith. "Of course, Chad was open every play. Once, we threw it to him for about 30 yards. It was a streak play, because at the time, what Chad mostly did was run fast and straight ahead.

"After that play, he'd come back in the huddle every play and say, 'They can't cover me.' We kept running the streak, he kept saying he was open."

Did you keep throwing him the ball?

"I didn't say that," Smith said.

Johnson's technique wasn't yet the best. "Chad would catch the ball and fall down a lot. 'Crash landing,' we called it," said Craig Austin, the offensive coordinator. But Johnson's diligence was impressive. Charles Collins began tutoring him on his balance and his footwork, and his route-running. Eventually, Collins' influence would expand considerably. He'd be teaching Johnson about much more than catching footballs.

Collins spent all of 1998 with Johnson. Johnson had lots of

time that year. His grades were so bad, he was ineligible to play football. That year, he took a job at a clothing store at the Fox Hills Mall, in nearby Culver City, giving him access to the latest in fashion. Not that Johnson took advantage of it.

During that season, the ineligible member of the Fab Five came to every Corsairs home game. Johnson would time his arrival for the second quarter, for maximum visibility. During a timeout, he'd walk in through the players gate, behind one of the goalposts, wearing leisure suits the colors of tropical fruit drinks.

"Miami suits," Steve Smith would call them, years later.

"Banana suits," said Dylen Smith.

"Lime green," Robert Taylor remembered. "Pink, yellow, brown. All with a matching hat."

"Walkers," was Johnson's description.

"Who's that guy in the ugly suit?" Taylor recalls his brother asking him.

"That's Chad Johnson," Taylor said. "We don't pay him any attention."

Chad would make his way to the Corsairs sideline.

"Coach, I'm here," he'd say.

"I'm coaching, Chad. Don't bother me. You going to class?"

"Yeah, coach. You want me to get you one of these suits?"

The year off benefited Johnson in many ways, if not sartorially. He got the alone time, daily, with Collins, who was already regarded as a premier teacher of wide receivers. He also realized, for the first time, how something he loved—something he had staked his life on—could be taken away.

"I was up his ass. For him to be eligible in '99, he had to do some things in summer school. I remember saying to him, 'I'm looking at your transcript. You'll probably never play football again. Go get a job,'" said Taylor.

"I'm gonna get it right, coach," Johnson said. And he did, showing up to practice at the start of the '99 season with a 2.0 grade-point. "Every time the chips were down with him, he came through," said Robert Taylor.

Said Johnson years later, "It almost took me failing to realize how serious it was."

Not more than a year later, Taylor would have his vacation interrupted by Dennis Erickson's phone calls. Erickson, the coach at Oregon State, where Johnson had signed to play, wanted to know if Johnson would be finishing summer school in time to make it to Oregon State's preseason workouts. "I told you, you have to watch him twenty-four hours a day," Taylor said to Erickson.

In fact, Johnson had failed a spring quarter course at Santa Monica, forcing him to miss spring practice at Oregon State. Again, he thought about quitting. Paula Johnson, among others, pushed him to register for the summer session. "We got him back for that final quarter, and he got his associate's degree," Paula said, years later. "The NFL is not the highlight of my life for him. It's him opening that book. When he went to the airport (to fly to Oregon State), we were both in tears. All I could say was, 'I'm proud of you.' I just kept saying it."

The Fab Five's run ended soon enough. Stevonne Smith moved smoothly from SMC to Utah to the first round of the NFL draft. The 5-foot-9 Smith grew up in the gang-infected area of South Central Los Angeles. "When we got him, he was an angry young man," said Robert Taylor. Taylor once asked Smith who he was mad at, since Smith seemed mad all the time. Smith couldn't answer that. Taylor decided Smith wouldn't play again until he answered the question.

On the surface, Chad Johnson and Stevonne Smith could not

have been more different. Chad was rarely serious; Stevonne rarely wasn't. Chad loved attention; Stevonne discouraged it. Chad blew off school. Stevonne knew he needed the grades to get out. Yet the two shared a desperate need to play football, and the equally desperate realization that football was all they had.

Each took the bus to school. Each remembers the bumps along the way. Whenever he visits Los Angeles now, Smith makes sure to drive past the Taco Bell in West L.A., where he worked during his high school and SMC days. "I just sit there and look at the place," Smith told *The New York Times*. "I knew it wasn't what I wanted to do with my life. I knew I was going to need a lot of determination and persistence to do something else."

The other three Fabs, and the quarterback Dylen Smith, all had professional football aspirations. Whether for lack of talent or ambition or luck, or combination thereof, none reached those heights. Success is fragile, ephemeral and can come without reason.

Eugene Sykes, at 5' 8", was the same size as Steve Smith. Sykes went from Santa Monica to Abilene Christian, where he led the team in receiving until the quarterback got hurt. The offense went conservative then, and Sykes' skills went mostly unused.

"I tried to stay in shape," he says now. "I ended up playing Arena ball in Fresno for a year. I had people saying, 'What are you doing here? You should be in the League.' It didn't work out in Fresno. I was disappointed. I was 31 years old. That was 2002. That was the end of it."

Sykes still believes he can play in the NFL. "At times, I want to ask Chad, 'Can you pull some strings for me?'" Instead, Eugene Sykes works at an Alcoa plant in Torrance, California, and still lives in South Central Los Angeles.

Dylen Smith tore his rotator cuff twice while trying to play professionally in Canada. Last year, he suffered a torn biceps on his throwing arm. He had surgery in December. While he still feels he can play, he's realistic enough to say, "I think that's it." He's the quarterbacks coach and assistant offensive coordinator at Malibu High School. Recently, Smith applied for a position with the Los Angeles County Sheriff's Department. He still lives in Santa Monica.

Demetrius Posey's is the saddest story of all. Posey had a scholarship to Utah, but his grades weren't good enough to qualify. He was big and strong, with great hands and a veteran's ability to run proper pass routes. "You could learn to be a complete player just by watching him," said Eugene Sykes.

In the off-season after his second year at Santa Monica College, Demetrius Posey apparently fell asleep at the wheel on his way back from Tijuana, Mexico. The crash killed him instantly.

Years later, Chad Johnson becomes quiet at the memory. "Shouldn't have happened to Posey. He should be playing with me and Steve," is the most he'll offer.

That, and this:

"When I got to Santa Monica, I wasn't any better than any of the other receivers there. It just mattered more to me. I needed guidance, though. I knew where I wanted to go, but I didn't know how to get there. I had to have someone to help me with that."

That would be Charles Collins.

"My guardian angel," Johnson said.

THE GUARDIAN

*E*ven after a promising, if erratic first season at Santa Monica College—Chad Johnson was nothing in those days if not erratic—the jury was still out on this kid from Miami with the gold teeth and the strangely colored suits.

He was the same "straight up clown," as his hometown mentor Terrence "T-Dog" Craig put it, that he'd been his whole life. Moving west hadn't changed anything about Chad Johnson but his address. The issue remained: Would the clown ever take off his makeup and fright wig long enough to learn how to play?

Ability was never a problem. Nor was his passion for football, not from the day as a 4-year-old when he first put on shoulder pads. It was his willingness to put in the time that was debatable, whether it was listening to coaching or going to class. The straight-up clown had an attention-deficit issue.

"The last person I'd have ever thought would make the

THE COACH'S CLASSROOM — WORKING OUT WITH COLLINS.

League" was SMC quarterback Dylen Smith's appraisal of his fast-running, fast-talking, live-wire wideout. "He was cocky, doing his own thing."

What had held Johnson back in high school dogged him at Santa Monica. It wasn't enough that after his senior year at Miami Beach High, he'd needed to take night summer school courses just to graduate. Nor did it suffice that his grandmother would not allow him to come home to Liberty City after he was dismissed from his first junior college, Langston College in Oklahoma, for fighting.

Johnson didn't make the grades at Santa Monica College, either. He was placed on academic probation after his freshman season, in 1997. He thought about giving up then, too. Again, Bessie Mae Flowers wouldn't let him.

That's when Charles Collins saved his life.

"He reminded me of myself. Young. All this energy, knows it all."

Collins knew a lot about lives in need of saving, or at least nudging. He grew up in South Central Los Angeles. In some ways, he was the stereotypical urban kid: poor, black, raised by a single mother in a neighborhood beginning to fester with gangs, drugs, and violence.

In other ways, Collins was different. As he and others explain it, when you grow up poor in a violent neighborhood, the road only goes two ways, right or wrong. You can choose to do one or the other, and the rest of your life is likely to be defined by that simple decision.

"Sports kept me out of the gangs," he recalled recently. "It gave me the push that was needed; it allowed me to work with people from different walks of life. Sports gives you that grind of getting knocked down and getting back up.

"I know that in the inner city, you have to have support to make it. At the end of the day, that support is everything. These kids have a chance to do something, to be something, if you just give them a little help."

No one understood this bit of wisdom better than Chad Johnson. In Liberty City, Sam Johnson, who ran the Optimist football program, has provided it to thousands of kids. Football coach Jim Kroll doled out support and second chances at Miami Beach High like they were hall passes. Bessie Mae once advised Charles Collins, "Don't give up on Chad. Just tell him you're giving up on him. He'll come around."

Collins had needed a mentor, too, someone with a gentle hand on his back. He turned to James Lofton. "Lofton was the one who raised the bar," Collins said, years later. Lofton grew up in the neighborhood, graduated from Washington High School, then went to Stanford on a football scholarship before having a Pro Bowl career in the National Football League.

In the off-season, Lofton trained at Southwest College, in L.A. That's where Charles Collins met him. Lofton impressed Collins immediately as someone who had a vision for himself, not just for today, but for a lifetime.

"This was a guy from the inner city who had a plan," Collins recalled. "He had a solid work ethic, a formula for success. His life had structure. He just seemed to do all the right things. I adopted all that. I could see the edge it gave me."

Collins says that all the great athletes in Los Angeles know each other, and train together. He began training with Lofton. Collins graduated from Manual Arts High, then went on to play wide receiver at Cal State Northridge. "I was considered a player," Collins says now. "As it turned out, I was a better teacher."

Meanwhile, his mother kept everything together at home. She raised three children alone, working various jobs. She was a nurse for awhile. She was a housekeeper in BelAir, a posh section west of the city, home to actors and entertainers. "She gave me that foundation, that stability," Collins recalled.

It was no wonder, then, that in this gifted, wayward wide receiver from Miami, he saw the kid he once was. As Collins says now, "He reminded me of myself. Young. All this energy, knows it all."

The first time Charles Collins sized up Chad Johnson, he said, "This kid is raw, but he has a chance. He loves to play, but he never will unless he takes care of business. I'm gonna take a chance on him, though, and either he proves me wrong or we'll get this done."

As with others who'd taken special interest in him—Bessie Mae, Terrence Craig, Jim Kroll, Robert Taylor—Johnson couldn't get enough of Charles Collins. It wasn't just that he'd found another father figure who'd taken a keen interest in him. Collins went deeper. He understood who Johnson was, why he acted how he did, and how to steer him in the right direction.

Others looked at Johnson's clowning and saw a cocky preener who lacked the discipline to be as good as he talked. Collins saw an insecure kid who needed the singular attention of someone who believed in him. "And," said Collins, "I was right."

It wasn't easy. With Johnson, it rarely is. Even now, three times a Pro Bowler and regarded as among the best wide receivers in the NFL, Chad Johnson can still be that insecure, wayward child. Collins began mentoring him in 1998, the year he was ineligible at Santa Monica College. He hasn't stopped.

"I'm not letting you be who you want to be no more," was Collins' first message.
"You're playing like you're in the park."

That's why Bengals receivers coach Hue Jackson asked Collins to talk to Johnson before the disastrous playoff game with the Pittsburgh Steelers last January, and again during Johnson's halftime meltdown. It's the reason Collins has been "up Chad's behind," as he puts it, every step of the way.

It's why Collins was thrust occasionally into Johnson's home life, away from football. Like Robert Taylor before him, Collins took calls from Bessie Mae Flowers in Miami and Chad's mother Paula Johnson, in nearby Baldwin Hills. Paula Johnson had called Taylor, the SMC head coach, more than once, asking his advice on handling her son.

"Do you have someplace for him to live?" Taylor recalls her asking him. "He has been terrible. I want him to move out."

Taylor talked with Chad. "What's wrong with you? You have one mama on this earth. She's letting you live in her house. Treat her right."

Collins recalls similar chats with his star pupil. "I dealt with all the mama drama," is how Collins puts it today.

It's why, during halftime of Cincinnati's season opener in 2004, Johnson was in the visiting locker room at Giants Stadium in East Rutherford, N.J., when his cell phone started to vibrate. The Bengals were playing the New York Jets. It was the debut of their second-year quarterback, Carson Palmer. Two years earlier, Palmer had been the first pick of the entire National Football League draft.

Possessing size, arm strength, and a football intelligence that could not be taught, Palmer was seen as a can't-miss star. Bengals coach Marvin Lewis had determined Palmer would not play his rookie season, preferring he learn from the sidelines, stay healthy, and watch veteran Jon Kitna lead the team.

That was 2003. Now, Palmer was The Man. The future had arrived. In the first half against the New York Jets, the future looked shaky. Palmer might eventually be the savior of this perpetually sad franchise. At the moment, he was a kid quarterback, making his first NFL start, and it showed.

Chad Johnson does not wear his emotions on his sleeve. His

sleeve doesn't have enough space. During a first half in which Palmer misfired in Johnson's direction or, worse, failed to recognize that Johnson, according to Johnson, was open every play, the wide receiver made it obvious he was irritated with his new QB.

On the field, Johnson waved his arms in disgust. On the sideline, helmet off, his irritation visited his face. Athletes have a term for this: Showing people up. It's frowned upon.

In California, Charles Collins was watching the game on TV. He saw his star pupil acting out. He was not amused. He picked up the telephone. "I called (Johnson's cell phone) four times," Collins recalled. "It was vibrating a lot, I'm sure."

A lot happens at halftime of an NFL game. Most of it involves coaches speaking, either to try to quick-fix what had gone wrong in the first half or to motivate players for the second half. Players don't do much talking at halftime. And they really don't talk on their cell phones. Johnson took his vibrating telephone into the locker room lavatory.

"I jawed at him for thirty hard seconds," Collins says now. "He reminded me of that kid I first met."

The conversation was strictly one-way. It went like this, teacher to student: "Be a pro. As blessed as you are, and you clown like that? Are you crazy? You're a veteran. You should be supporting Palmer. Instead, you're rattling him. If you ever pull some T.O. shit like that again, I will come up there and embarrass you," said Collins, a reference to NFL wideout Terrell Owens, a great player whose me-first histrionics have overshadowed his talent.

That sort of father-son maintenance started from the first day Collins and Johnson were together. SMC offensive coordinator Craig Austin had told Collins, "We have a kid you need to coach. He don't listen to us." Collins got Johnson's attention, if only because Johnson knew, again, he was running out of last chances. "He had nothing but football, and he knew I was his last straw," said Collins.

Johnson also knew, even then, that Collins knew what he was talking about. Collins had worked with Chad's cousin, Keyshawn Johnson, the former USC star who'd become a very good player in the NFL.

Collins had trained with James Lofton and worked with Isaac Bruce, another Santa Monica College alumnus, who'd gone on to win Pro Bowl status and a Super Bowl ring with the St. Louis Rams. Years later, Collins' success with Johnson—and Johnson's success in the NFL—would launch in earnest Collins' career as wide receiver coach to the stars and would-be stars. Theirs has been a mutually beneficial and lucrative relationship.

In 1998, it was just a coach looking at a kid with bad grades and lots of passion for football.

"I'm not letting you be who you want to be no more," was Collins' first message. "You're playing like you're in the park." The more Johnson hung around his new coach, the more he wanted to hang around him. Today, Collins estimates they were together "320 of the 365 days" of the year Johnson was academically ineligible to play football at Santa Monica College. "I didn't give him much time to get into anything," Collins says.

At first, they worked on everything. Johnson had a habit of leaving his feet, on even the simplest catches, and falling down, a trait his SMC coaches laid on his need to be theatrical. Collins hit all the wide-receiving basics: Leverage on defensive backs, and separation from them; timing; balance. "I defeated him with knowledge," Collins recalls.

It wasn't hard. Johnson was as passionate for football as he was apathetic for schoolwork. He never missed a training session with

Collins. In fact, he'd often be the one initiating the drills. Collins can't recall now how many times his pupil woke him up on a Sunday morning, wanting to work.

"I don't think he wanted to disappoint me, or his grandmother," Collins explains. "Wherever I went, he went. It became more like a father-son relationship. I was that figure who put that no-nonsense into him."

"Coach C," as Johnson still calls Collins, devoted all of 1998 to coaching Johnson. "What made him ready to play at the next level was how I coached him. He got me alone. It was a mental evolution for him," Collins said.

Playing wide receiver is more than running fast and

holding onto the ball. The details of playing the position at a high level, the way Johnson has done for the past three years in the NFL, are fodder for another chapter. Basically, Charles Collins taught Chad Johnson how to be a pass receiver, not simply a football player who runs fast.

He's still doing it. During the last week of March 2006, Collins visited Johnson in Miami, to brush up his star student's fundamentals after more than two months of inactivity. "Chad still has a tendency just to go out there and run and jump. To be too cute. 'Hollywood,' I call it. We emphasize being consistent, not deviating from technique," said Collins.

Collins also calls Johnson frequently, especially in the off-season. After a month off, he expects Johnson to resume low-impact training. "If you never get out of shape, you don't have to worry about getting into shape. There was always a method to my madness, so when you get to camp you are that much better than everyone else," said Collins.

Between the Bengals' spring minicamps and the opening of training camp in July, Johnson and Collins will be working together nearly every day. Some things don't change. Some relationships don't fade.

Johnson sees two guardian angels in his life: his grandmother and Coach C. Each saw something in him others did not. No one knows him better. "To get where I want to go, I have to be consistent," Johnson says. "I have to do the same things year after year, only better. Catching the ball, blocking, running the right routes, being where I'm supposed to be. Acting like a veteran."

It was Charles Collins who taught him that, having been taught the same by James Lofton. After he left Cal State Northridge, Collins played four years in the Canadian Football League, bypassing a tryout with the San Diego Chargers to sign a

$300,000 contract to play up north. "I look at some of the guys I coach now, and I think I could have been them," he says.

Instead, he has run since 2002 a flourishing wide receiver camp in L.A., called the Phenom Factory. Among his clients are Johnson and his teammates, T.J. Houshmandzadeh and Antonio Chapman; and Steve Smith of the Carolina Panthers.

Collins also has designed an under-the-uniform garment he calls the "HitProof" compression suit, a one-pound, one-piece microfiber suit that provides protection without hindering mobility.

Much of Chad Johnson's success he owes to Charles Collins. Likewise, Collins has been able to trade on Johnson's fame to amp his business. The relationship has matured into something that benefits both men.

When Johnson first trained with Collins, the coach would not permit his student to wear his gold teeth. Collins offers unique insight into his student's ongoing, on-field antics: "Chad really doesn't know how to be a celebrity. That's what people have put on him. I have to remind him where not to go with it. But one thing I've always enjoyed about him is that he does have a level of humility. He understands he didn't get to where he is without a lot of help. And he repays that."

Collins won't hesitate to set Johnson straight, however. Johnson still needs that, from time to time.

That's what father figures are for.

PREPARATION

The Cincinnati Bengals were already horrible in 2002, before Chad Johnson dropped the pass that launched his career toward stardom.

By October 4, when they played the Colts in Indianapolis, the Bengals were 0-4, on their way to 2-14. You'd have sparked an endless debate in Cincinnati by asking which Bengals club was the worst in franchise history: This '02 crew? Or the 3-13 bunch of 1993, "led" by David Klingler and Harold Green, coached by Dave Shula? Because the Bengals were the Bengals, you could have enlarged the debate to suggest that one of these teams was, by extension, the worst club in the post-merger history of the National Football League.

Unlike the '93 team, which was outscored by 132 points and whose leading receiver was someone named Jeff Query, the '02 team was not without talent. After playing the first four

games with Gus Frerotte at quarterback, the Bengals settled on Jon Kitna, whose leadership and accountability quickly won over his teammates. Corey Dillon would run for 1,311 yards. Young veteran linebackers Takeo Spikes and Brian Simmons were developing nicely. As was Chad Johnson, the second-year wideout.

He had lots to learn, though. As a rookie, Johnson had played behind second-year man Peter Warrick and eight-year veteran Darnay Scott. All the potential Johnson showed as a rookie in spring camp and during the season was still just that. As Jon Kitna noted, "That first year, I didn't want him on the field with me. He would do the wrong thing. He didn't care. He didn't want to put in the extra time. He was supposed to be running a slant route, he'd run an out."

All the time spent with Charles Collins had not yet translated into lessons learned. It would, though. All it took was one play.

With thirty-one seconds left against the Colts, the winless Bengals trailed just 28-21 and looked to have a chance. In his first start after replacing Frerotte, Kitna had moved the Bengals offense. Kitna had been the starter the previous season, but he'd thrown 22 interceptions and just 12 touchdowns, so the Bengals opted to sign Frerotte as a free agent, and hand him the starting job to begin 2002. In Frerotte's four starts, Cincinnati scored 23 points. The team turned again to Kitna.

'You can't go talking like that in the papers, and then do what you just did.'

"When Brat told me I would be starting," Kitna recalled years later, referring to offensive coordinator Bob Bratkowski, "I told him I wanted Chad starting with me."

Kitna's relationship with the young wide receiver was forever

"You can be so much better than ninety-five percent of the guys who play this game...You can be a superstar."—Kitna to Johnson

changed that day, but it wasn't the first time the pair had crossed paths. Johnson missed four games as a rookie, after breaking his collarbone making a catch in an October game. When he came back, Johnson let it be known that Kitna shouldn't be the Bengals quarterback any longer than necessary.

"He said something like, 'We got a Cadillac and we're putting the wrong gas in it,'" said Kitna. The Caddy being Johnson. "We played in Baltimore the next Sunday. Chad had chances to have a 99-yard touchdown, a 75-yarder, and a 35. He dropped the 99 and the 75, and he let the cornerback squeeze him on the 35-yarder.

Earlier in the game, Johnson had been running a slant, but broke off the pattern. The result was an interception that would be counted against Kitna, but was Johnson's fault.

"I just lost it on him on the sidelines. I said, 'You can't go talking like that in the papers, and then do what you just did.' We had to be separated. We were almost to blows."

The following Wednesday, Kitna apologized to Johnson for taking the argument public, but not about what he had said. "That's not what I meant," Johnson said, hoping to explain the 'Cadillac' comment.

"I don't care what you meant," said Kitna. "You can't do that in this league. They're always looking for a way to create controversy. If you insist on doing that, you can't drop balls."

Kitna and Johnson both say that was the end of their anger toward one another. Kitna, a deeply religious man who preferred leading by example, was not comfortable getting up in players' faces. Johnson appreciated it, however, saying years later, "I didn't have anyone in that locker room to learn from. Nobody taught me how to be a professional. We didn't have strong veteran

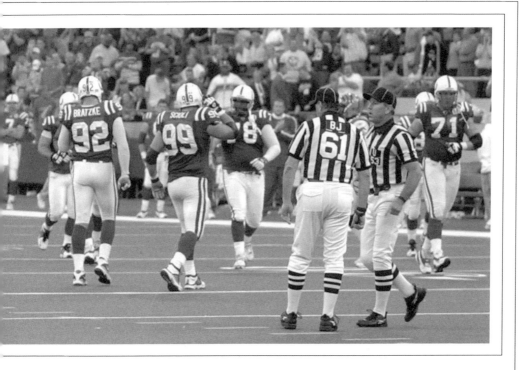

leadership, so I had to learn it on my own. Kitna was the first guy to set me straight."

The Bengals were driving against Indy, hoping to win their first game of the 2002 season. With thirty-one seconds to go, Kitna saw Johnson running deep and free across the Colts secondary. Earlier in the game, Johnson had been running a slant, but broke off the pattern. The result was an interception that would be counted against Kitna, but was Johnson's fault.

Now, redemption was at hand. Kitna threw a perfect strike. Johnson, perhaps surprised to be so open so late in a close game, took his eye off the ball a split second. The pass hit him in the helmet, bounced away, and was intercepted. Game over, defeat complete.

To anyone who had watched Cincinnati Bengals football for the previous, Lost Decade, this was yet another example of what had become known as a Bengal Moment.

Johnson was inconsolable in the locker room. Recalled Kitna, "It was almost like someone in his family had died. A serious emotional outburst." Other Bengals were telling Kitna not to baby Johnson, just to leave him alone. Kitna thought the moment was overwhelmingly significant. He would be proven right, year after year. So right that Johnson says now that when—not if, when—he is elected to the Pro Football Hall of Fame, he will credit what Kitna said to him that day as a reason for his enshrinement.

"I have more confidence in you after this game than I ever have," Kitna began. "You can be so much better than ninety-five percent of the guys who play this game. You have the opportunity not just to be good. You can be a superstar.

"But this is a defining moment. You're going to go one of two ways. You're going to decide it's not going to matter to you, it's not worth it, and you'll be out of the league in a couple years. Or you're going to go the other way and be a superstar."

Years later, Chad Johnson would say, "That was all it took right there. From that day, I dedicated myself. Do the work and the rest takes care of itself."

In most ways, the loss to Indianapolis was typical of the Lost Decade: Corey Dillon ran well, 164 yards; a new quarterback offered initial optimism that proved fleeting; Cincinnati's 26th-ranked defense gave up too many points; the Bengals committed six penalties and four turnovers, and found a way to lose.

The rest of the year was a downbound train, no different than the ten years before it. Players griped about a lack of leadership. A wideout named Michael Westbrook, signed in the off-season as a free agent, declared himself after the fourth game "the best player out there," then was removed from the active roster the following week. Westbrook responded to that Sunday morning demotion by walking out of Paul Brown Stadium soon before kickoff.

After a home loss to Pittsburgh plunged the Bengals to 0-6, a photo in the *Dayton Daily News* showed a Cincinnati fan wearing a bag over his head. "WE WANT KLINGLER" was scrawled on the bag. (David Klingler, a notorious first-round draft pick flop, hadn't played for Cincinnati since 1995.) A letter writer to the *Cincinnati Enquirer* suggested the city's name be purged from any and all things Bengal, so as not to cause the town any further embarrassment.

Even the hardiest of Bengals fans were dropping like dead flies off the bandwagon, which, by 2002, came with an odor all its own. Team radio man Dave Lapham, arguably the Last True Believer among Bengals fans, said this, to the *Enquirer* on October 6, 2002:

"It's Groundhog Day. I hear myself saying the same things I said eight years ago. Over and over. A month into the season, I'm freakin' fried already."

Not everything was sky-is-falling disastrous. Chad Johnson had started coming to practice early and staying late. He volunteered to practice on special teams. He asked to be on the "scout team," the group of players, almost always reserves, who mimicked the upcoming opponent's offense and defense. Anything to build his stamina.

After the Indianapolis game, Johnson had said to Kitna, "I just get so tired out there, I can't focus." Kitna told him the only remedy was to go harder in practice.

"That's when he started practicing like a pro," Kitna recalled. The quarterback had said one other thing, too, after the loss to the Colts. It would prove prophetic:

"If he does it right, he's going to look back at this game and say, 'That's the game that propelled me to greatness.'"

Fast forward to September 2005. Chad Johnson is sitting in

the living room of his Cincinnati condominium. It is 8 o'clock on a Tuesday morning. Frank Sinatra is on the boombox in the kitchen: "Fly Me to the Moon."

Two days earlier, the Bengals had beaten the Bears in Chicago, to begin their season 3-0. Chad Johnson caught two touchdown passes from Carson Palmer. They were the difference in a difficult, conservative game. The Bears dropped to 1-2 with the loss but, thanks to their outstanding defense, would finish the season well, and make the playoffs. On this day, though, it was largely the Chad and Carson Show.

It wasn't an accident. It wasn't even because Chad Johnson possesses the speed, the balance, and the body control that even some of the better NFL wideouts dream of having.

It was the preparation.

It was Johnson, taking the knowledge of Charles Collins and the advice of Jon Kitna, combining it with his own passion for the game, and running with it the length of the field.

Before he could be a great wide receiver, he had to be a smart one. "You have to understand what the defense is trying to do to you," Kitna had told him. What makes Johnson better than most—superior to that "ninety-five percent" Kitna talked about—is his willingness to do the drudgery of scouting his opponents.

"People think I just go out and play and talk," Johnson said in the fall of 2005. "They don't understand the work I put in to be able to do that."

By the 2003 season, Johnson was spending Wednesday nights, and occasionally Thursday nights, in the players lounge at Paul Brown Stadium. Videotape had been broken down by the Bengals' coaches and distributed to players. Johnson would get his tapes of the upcoming opponent's defensive players, then curl up on the leather couch and watch them, again and again, seeking tendencies and flaws in the opposing defensive backs' coverage techniques. Johnson spent so much time watching tape, he found it easier just to sleep at the stadium.

The team gives players CDs now, so by '04 Johnson was watching at home. The week after the Bears game, he explained in detail how he was able to score twice against Chicago's talented secondary.

The first TD pass was a post pattern. Johnson runs straight a designated number of yards, depending on the pattern called, then slants at a 45-degree angle toward the goal post. The Bengals were already inside the Bears' 20-yard line. Johnson lines up, sees Chicago cornerback Charles Tillman is playing slightly to Johnson's outside (right) shoulder. The Bears' corners like to funnel the opposing team's receivers toward the middle, where Chicago's Pro Bowl safety, Mike Brown, roams. Brown has a considerable nose for the ball. He's also a vicious hitter, something in the back of every wide receiver's mind when he's running across the middle of the field.

Tillman is lined up 8 yards off Johnson, a concession to Johnson's speed. The last thing Tillman wants is for Johnson to get behind him. When the ball is snapped, Johnson uses his speed to attack Tillman and get him off balance. Johnson runs right at Tillman then, at the last, split second, dips his right shoulder ever so slightly toward Tillman's outside shoulder.

"That made him widen just a little bit, an inch," Johnson explains. Johnson is animated, feinting and juking in the living room of his condo. "When he did that, I slipped underneath, toward the goal post. Not toward Mike Brown in the middle."

Johnson called the pattern a "skinny post," meaning he didn't take the full 45 degrees. If he'd done that, Brown would have been waiting for him, malice in his heart.

He comes in early and stays late and thinks about it all the time in between. Now, defenses designing their game plans for the Bengals begin the discussion with how they're going to neutralize Chad Johnson.

"They're trying to run me toward Mike Brown, but I stayed high." The slight dip of his right shoulder had forced Charles Tillman to lean to the outside.

"Just that little crack was all I needed to get where I needed to go," Johnson said.

Carson Palmer threw a perfect pass. Tillman was a step behind and to the outside; Brown hadn't had time to reach Johnson, who'd lessened the angle.

Touchdown.

"You get that from looking at film," said Johnson. "You see what they want to do to you. Anyone else would have been laid out by Brown. But I knew what to do. If I lean too soon, that pass is broken up. It's a matter of an inch, and I knew it was going to be like that. I studied."

ESPN's football show "Playmakers" is playing on the big screen in Johnson's living room as he's talking. Not long after Johnson explains the touchdown, ESPN's Sean Salisbury appears on TV, to break down the play. "The corner thinks he's forcing Chad inside, so the safety can come over and knock Chad in the mouth. What Chad Johnson does is, he leans and keeps the corner here." Salisbury points to the outside, near the sideline. "The corner jumps and completely misses."

"Watch my right shoulder," Johnson says, watching himself on TV.

"Playmaking made easy," Salisbury says. "Especially when Chad Johnson is your wide receiver."

Later, the game still in doubt, Johnson streaked by Chicago's other corner, Nathan Vasher, to haul in a 40-yard bomb that clinched the win. Seconds earlier, Bengals wide receivers coach Hue Jackson had said to Johnson on the sideline, "It's time for a big player to make a big play."

"Playmaking made easy," ESPN's Sean Salisbury says.
"Especially when Chad Johnson is your wide receiver."

"People think I just go out and play and talk," Johnson said in the fall of 2005. "They don't understand the work I put in to be able to do that."

The pattern Johnson ran for the second score was a simple Go route: Take off. Run fast, run straight. The sort of play Johnson had performed a thousand times, ever since his first day of practice at Santa Monica College. But in the NFL, there is more to a successful Go pattern than simply speed. Players and coaches call it "creating separation" between yourself and the defensive back.

Johnson looked at Vasher, across the line. He could see Vasher up on the balls of his feet. Johnson recalled something Deion Sanders had told him, namely to look at a cornerback's feet as you line up. If he's flat-footed, he isn't going to jam you at the line of scrimmage. "You can't play DB on your toes," Johnson explains. You have to be flat-footed to move left and right."

He knew Vasher was preparing to play bump-and-run coverage. "I knew the jam was coming. As soon as the ball was snapped, he came at me. I knew he'd aim for my shoulder pads," said Johnson. Coverage technique diagnosed, all Johnson had to do was duck a shoulder. "I came off (the line) like I was little. I ducked. He didn't have any place to hit me. He missed me, I was past him, and it was over. We got that second touchdown and it was a wrap."

His evolution as a wide receiver continues, if only because Johnson himself is never satisfied.

"Football is his passion," Jon Kitna said, late in the 2005 season. "That Indy game, he decided he wanted to be the best. Before that, he was like, 'I made it. I'm here.' He had over 100 yards receiving. (Actually, Johnson caught six balls that day, for 72 yards.) He could have had 200. That was my point."

The straight-up clown takes one thing entirely seriously. He comes in early and stays late and thinks about it all the time in between. Now, defenses designing their game plans for the Bengals begin the discussion with how they're going to neutralize Chad Johnson.

"There are four or five ways teams try to take Chad away," Kitna said. "That's our number one question, as an offense, every week. Which one will they choose? There's always that feeling-out process at the beginning of the game: OK, this is what they're going to do with Chad, this is how we attack it."

Johnson spends part of every off-season with his guru, Charles Collins, working on technique and understanding further what defensive backs want to do to throw him off. As Hue Jackson put it, "You don't do what he's done by not understanding defenses and doing your homework. His greatest gift is route-running. He understands how to create separation, how to sink his hips, how to get out of breaks fast."

Back in the condo, Sean Salisbury is on ESPN, telling the world that Chad Johnson is more than end zone dances and outrageous pronouncements.

"He knows football," Johnson remarked. "He must have played."

A visitor informs Johnson that Salisbury was a quarterback at the University of Southern California.

"For real?" Johnson asked.

The man
MARVIN

*H*is phone will hum. Any time, night or day, during the season, during the off-season, three o'clock in the morning. The phone will be on the nightstand next to the bed, and it will hop from the vibration. Chad Johnson is calling Marvin Lewis.

"Coach, what you doin'?"

"It's three o'clock, Chad. I'm sleeping."

Lewis always keeps his phone on. Just in case something is really wrong.

"What are *you* doing?"

"Gettin' ready for the game," Johnson might say.

"Where are you, Chad?"

"C'mon, coach. I'm at home."

And he would be.

One of Chad Johnson's favorite jokes is to tell Marvin Lewis that he had been out on the town earlier in the evening, and had seen Lewis' daughter in a club. And that, he, Chad, was always home before the coach's college-age daughter, Whitney, was.

"OK, Chad. That's good," Lewis might say. "Get some rest."

Johnson calls Lewis and Bengals wide receiver coach Hue Jackson a lot, often way after hours. Jackson often tells Johnson to be home by 12 a.m.—"Nothing good happens after midnight," is Jackson's message—and generally, Johnson is. The gregarious, outrageous performer on the field is a homebody off it.

It's that part of Johnson that most people don't see. It's the part that Lewis appreciates and respects. It allows the coach to tolerate the other Chad. Chad Johnson has a few father figures in his life, his former junior college position coach Charles Collins foremost among them. Hue Jackson plays the role, occasionally. Marvin Lewis does as well. The coach regards Johnson as a wayward son, the precocious 12-year-old he wants to swat and hug, often at the same time.

"I hope I'm fatherly to him," Lewis said last winter. "There is a great concern from my boss (Bengals owner Mike Brown) that Chad Johnson be able to function after football, financially and as a person. I see it as part of our charge."

Johnson pays tribute to Lewis. The coach, Johnson says, has taught him how to be a professional. "It's all Coach Lew," says Johnson. "Everything we've done the last three years. The way we practice. The way we work out in the off-season. The way we study. He has taught us how to win."

"We are beginning to learn that this is a team game. It's not the Chad Johnson Show...."

Lewis has had his moments with Johnson. Lewis worked for Bill Cowher in Pittsburgh, where he learned the importance of selflessness and how powerful one unified team with one shared goal could be. The Steelers under Cowher have never led the league in Look At Me. They've done their talking on the field, usually with their shoulder pads in your ribs.

Lewis learned, too, how one personality can be infectious, especially if it belongs to a great player. As Baltimore's defensive coordinator for six years, he saw how middle linebacker Ray Lewis became the Ravens' best player and spiritual heart. Ray Lewis, whom Marvin Lewis nicknamed "Big Play," was not subtle in his play or his persona. Ray Lewis let the world know he was in the house. So while Marvin Lewis hasn't been crazy about his loud wideout's Guarantees and Lists and general candor, he has been cautious in reining it in.

"The only time he ever said anything to me was after I made the guarantee," said Johnson. In 2003, the week before the 4-5 Bengals hosted the 9-0 Kansas City Chiefs, Johnson said the Bengals would win: "Some people may not like the guarantee, but I know my teammates are not going to leave me hanging."

One who didn't like it was across the locker room. Willie Anderson was an eight-year veteran in 2003, on his way to his first Pro Bowl. He was the most respected player in the locker room, hands down. "Chad's playing to get to the Pro Bowl and get a big paycheck," he said. "He's not a leader on this team. We rally behind guys who work hard and are subtle with their comments, guys like Rudi Johnson or Jon Kitna. Not the loudmouth guy who puts his gold teeth in before you go on the field."

The notion of Johnson as selfish grandstander has ebbed some as teammates have become accustomed (or immune) to his brash nature and grown respectful of his ability and work ethic. Yet more than two years after Anderson's rebuke of the guarantee, Johnson's teammates were saying much the same thing, privately, after the star receiver's well-publicized halftime explosion in the playoff game against Pittsburgh.

Lewis wasn't as miffed as Anderson about The Guarantee. He did tell Johnson that what he said had consequences beyond himself, and to consider the effect his words might have on others. Ironically, the same week Johnson guaranteed the win, the Bengals extended his contract, through the 2009 season. And they beat the Chiefs, 24-19.

The week before The Guarantee, Lewis lashed out publicly at Johnson, after Johnson was penalized for what the referees believed was a throat-slashing gesture, following a touchdown catch. The 15-yard violation prompted Lewis to say, after a 27-24 home win over the Seattle Seahawks, "We are beginning to learn that this is a team game. It's not the Chad Johnson Show. He was not trying to do what it came across that he was doing, but we don't need it either way. Play football."

Two years later, Johnson would enchant the media each week during the 2005 season with a greaseboard rendering of the names of the defensive backs he would face during the year. "The List," as he called it, had two boxes—Yes and No—beside each name, along with the question, "Who Covered 85 in '05?" The Yes box was checked just once all year, beside the name of Leigh Bodden. a cornerback for the Cleveland Browns. No one else covered Johnson all season, according to Johnson.

One week, Lewis expressed his view of The List by removing it from Johnson's locker and rewriting it. Lewis' List included different questions, all involving Johnson's abilities as a team player. This is a message coach has worked to impart to player since the pair joined forces in 2003. As much as anyone, Lewis understands that Johnson isn't a selfish player, just an excitable and occasionally overreaching one. As Hue Jackson puts it, "Chad's passion is always skewed by this: He thinks he can carry a team on his back."

Marvin Lewis was unlike any head coach the Bengals had ever hired. He was African-American, for one. More important, he was the first coach they'd brought in from outside the organization.

Figuring out what makes Chad tick has been easy for Lewis, compared to the overall task he faced when he was hired. Marvin Lewis' assignment was unlike any other in the National Football League. Not only did Lewis have to win. He had to teach his players how to win. None who had played any length of time for the Bengals had much of a clue.

When he accepted the job as Bengals head coach on January 14, 2003, Lewis didn't just inherit a losing football team. He acquired a losing culture, as deeply ingrained as any in sports. Twelve years without a winning season, twelve years without a playoff appearance. The worst record in the league during that time, 55-137. An image among players as the Siberia of the NFL. A place of last resort, for old players seeking a final paycheck and young players without alternatives. An old school owner seen as cheap and anachronistic, who had never adjusted to the free agent era.

NFL players are a close-knit fraternity. On any given weekend in the fall, there are only about 1,600 of them active, in the world. They see each other socially in the off-season. They talk. Nothing good was ever said about the Bengals.

The team seemed stuck perpetually in loss mode. Yet something was different about this hire. Something that bespoke of change and vibrancy and an optimism not seen since the late 1980s. Marvin Lewis was unlike any head coach the Bengals had ever hired. He was African-American, for one. More important, he was the first coach they'd brought in from outside the organization. The Bengals were notoriously inbred; Paul Brown hired his two sons, Mike and Pete. Mike Brown hired his daughter Katie, whose future husband, Troy Blackburn, would become the team's director of business development. Mike Brown hired his son Paul, the team's current vice president of player personnel.

When Lewis accepted the job as Bengals head coach on January 14, 2003, he didn't just inherit a losing football team. He acquired a losing culture, as deeply ingrained as any in sports.

From Sam Wyche to Dave Shula to Bruce Coslet to Dick LeBeau, Mike Brown kept his inner circle close, and gratefully obliging. One of the many criticisms of Bengals management during the twelve losing seasons was the perceived lack of creativity and new ideas. To Mike Brown, loyalty was more important than creativity. He felt safer in his authority when he knew he could keep his thumb on everyone who worked for him.

Marvin Lewis was nothing like that. He'd created a Super Bowl-winning defense in Baltimore in 2000, as the Ravens' defensive coordinator. He'd gone to the Washington Redskins in the same capacity in 2002, for what at the time was the largest salary ever paid an NFL assistant coach.

After the 2000 season, Lewis' name was on the short list whenever head coaching vacancies were discussed. He'd never made the final cut. Some had suggested he didn't interview well. That might have been the case elsewhere. It was not in Cincinnati. Lewis' vision and attention to detail wowed Katie and Troy Blackburn immediately. They had to sell Lewis to Mike Brown, who was partial to Tom Coughlin, the former Jacksonville Jaguars coach. Coughlin's rigid, my-way-or-the-highway approach impressed Brown, who had wearied of selfish star players seemingly running the team.

Brown also expressed considerable interest in Pittsburgh Steelers assistant Mike Mularkey. Ultimately, Brown accepted the counsel of his daughter and son-in-law. It was the first public suggestion that the owner who had drawn relentless criticism from Bengals fans for more than a decade was ready to relinquish some of his control.

The Bengals chose Lewis. But no more than he chose them. He saw it as an opportunity. He couldn't possibly do worse than his predecessors had and, unlike in almost any other NFL town, where the mandate to win came with a nearly instant expiration date, he knew he'd be given a grace period in Cincinnati.

Lewis did ask for certain concessions. One was a much greater say in player personnel matters. He'd seen how a perceived lack of clout had undermined Shula, Coslet, and LeBeau. If he were to take the job, he'd need to be able to keep players he liked and, more important, weed out those he didn't. While Lewis respected great ability, he was not beholden to it. Lewis would not let a player's talent be the deciding factor in his employment, if he believed that player would be disruptive.

The public would see that side of Lewis early on. Linebacker Takeo Spikes was the best player and emotional heart of the Bengals defense. While the Cincinnati defense was lousy annually, Spikes was not. He had led the team in tackles in four of his five seasons.

Three days after the Bengals hired Lewis, Spikes was telling the local papers he no longer wanted to play in Cincinnati. He wished Lewis well, but wasn't convinced the new coach would have any more power than his predecessors. The Bengals had been 19-61 in Spikes' five seasons; he was tired of losing: "Is it really going to change? I've told (Lewis) I don't want to be there. One bad apple can spoil the basket."

Publicly, Lewis was disappointed he couldn't convince Spikes to stay. Privately, the coach felt Spikes was not the great player Bengals fans, and Spikes himself, believed he was. Regardless, Lewis was not going to fool with players who didn't want to play for him. Spikes signed with the Buffalo Bills.

This sent a few messages out to Bengals fans and, more significantly, to current players. If Lewis could do without his best defensive player, nobody was safe. To fans, it suggested Mike Brown was serious about loosening his grip on the team.

If that were the case, Brown had picked the right man to assume control. Marvin Lewis grew up in McDonald, Pennsylvania, near Pittsburgh, where his father, Marvin Sr., spent his working career at the Shenango Foundry on Neville Island. Marvin Lewis Sr. spent so many years wielding a sledgehammer as a shift laborer, he'd have to prop his elbows on a pillow at night, to limit their throbbing.

There is something about the southwestern Pennsylvania mentality that lends itself to successfully playing and coaching football. There is a toughness in the region that persists to this day, even after most of the steel mills have shut down. It's a sleeves-rolled mindset, combined with an absolute lack of pretense. Hardheaded, hardworking people make great football players and coaches. Think Mike Ditka of Hopewell and Bill Cowher of Carlynton, and Marty Schottenheimer, not to mention Joe Namath, Joe Montana, Jim Kelly, Dan Marino, and Tony Dorsett. And Marvin Lewis, of McDonald.

He worked in a coke mill once, for nine weeks, just long enough to convince himself he didn't want to do that for the rest of his life. The ovens in the mill reached 2,800 degrees. They melted the frames of his glasses. "Nine weeks of hell," Lewis would recall, years later.

Other summers, he was a garbageman. You work these jobs while growing up, to make a little spending money and to learn what you didn't want to do forever. As a high school quarterback, Marvin Lewis spent his study hall time watching game film. When it came time for him to choose a career, he decided he wanted to be a coach, specifically a head coach in the NFL.

Marvin Sr. wasn't thrilled. It was the early 1980s. The elder Lewis considered the notion of a black NFL head coach to be the longest of shots. He'd hoped his son would become an engineer. The son's answer to the father was simple and borne of experience, his and his dad's: "I want to do what I love to do," he said.

One of the first things Lewis did as Bengals head coach was call a meeting of all the team's employees. He introduced his coaching staff. He had each department head introduce their staffs. Lewis' message: Everyone is important. A few weeks later, Lewis asked the team's public affairs director, Jeff Berding, for a list of Paul Brown Stadium suite holders.

The new coach sent each a letter, detailing his plan for the team. Not long after, he sent them another letter, linking their support and the team's ability to compete. He held a reception for major sponsors.

No detail escaped Lewis' notice. He upgraded the Bengals weight room, figuring if he were going to ask players to come to Cincinnati to lift in the off-season, he could at least make the work environment more pleasant.

In July, just before the start of his first training camp, Lewis stopped at the team's training site at Georgetown College, just outside Lexington, Kentucky. He was checking on the condition of the freshly planted grass. After walking the main practice field, Lewis would report that there were a few brown patches, and could someone please fix those?

Lewis liked to say that first summer, "You want to be a pro? We're here to help you." Another Lewis favorite, still often repeated: "I see better than I hear." He raised the team's professionalism immediately. "You're a professional athlete," Lewis said. "Don't have your pants sagging off your butt. If you want to hang with the guys on the corner, go ahead. We've got a lot of guys to replace you."

And they did. Lewis let a Lost Decade holdover named Reinard Wilson have it one day during practice. Wilson had been another dubious first-round draft pick, who hadn't respected his talent. One day that summer, Wilson shoved an offensive lineman into quarterback Shane Mathews. A strict training camp edict is that quarterbacks are not touched in practice. "You're selfish!" Lewis yelled at Wilson. "You don't care about the team. All you care about is yourself." Wilson, drafted in 1997, should have been in the prime of his career. He didn't make the team.

To foster improved relations with the fans, Lewis rarely said no to a public appearance. At training camp, he made available to players a box of Sharpies, the writing tool of choice for people seeking autographs. Lewis encouraged his players to sign as they walked off the practice field.

The Bengals began the '03 season in familiar fashion: They lost their first three games. They were 1-4 going into a home game with the Baltimore Ravens. The preseason optimism was giving way to Same Old Bengals nightmares.

Then the Bengals beat Baltimore 34-26, thanks in part to an 82-yard touchdown pass from Jon Kitna to Chad Johnson. The pass bounced off the shoulder pad of Ravens' safety Ed Reed, and into Johnson's hands.

Afterward Johnson explained he knew where the ball would bounce after it hit Reed. "The angle was going to bring it right to me," Johnson said. Longtime Bengals observers saw it differently. In previous sad seasons, that ball wouldn't have bounced off Ed Reed's shoulder; it would have popped off Johnson's head, same as that pass at Indianapolis had the previous, pre-Marvin year. Reed would have intercepted it.

The karma was definitely changing.

The Bengals would rally from the 1-4 start to finish 8-8. They would be in the playoff hunt up to the last game. Corey Dillon would challenge Marvin Lewis' authority. The team's all-time leading rusher would be traded to the New England Patriots for a second-round draft pick.

Mike Brown faded into the background. Marvin Lewis became coach and spokesman. As promised, Lewis also had a big say in personnel matters. Mike Brown would never have ridded himself of Takeo Spikes and Corey Dillon, no matter their gripes. But Lewis did.

Against that backdrop, Chad Johnson's game flourished. He had a head coach he believed in, and a position coach, Hue Jackson, he could trust and learn from. The bond between

Lewis and Johnson isn't always tight—Lewis believes in keeping a professional distance from his players; he disdains the term "players' coach"—but it's strong enough to have weathered some Johnson-made storms.

"He's a live-for-the-moment guy," Lewis said, "but he has become more aware of big-picture things. Relationships, financial things, things he can do off the field. He realizes he doesn't have it all figured out."

Lewis would like Johnson to become more of a leader, and to realize the effect his moods, good and bad, and his occasional outbursts, have on the team. "Him realizing the impact he has on the mental well-being of the team" is how the coach puts it.

Lewis has seen Johnson's soft side. One year, the coach attended the Ebony Fashion Fair, a show sponsored by *Ebony* magazine. He was impressed by the poise and confidence displayed by the runway models and wanted some of his players to see it. He decided to buy a table for the following year, and invited several Bengals to attend, Johnson among them.

"I asked them to wear black tie," Lewis recalled. "Chad was pleased I asked him to go, and that I told him how to dress. He thanked me. Inside that guy who celebrates touchdowns is a thoughtful kid, a good person." Lewis has taken Johnson with him to the annual dinner for the local Special Olympics chapter.

"The kids were mesmerized," said Lewis. "As Chad matures as a person, I hope we'll see more of that side of him, and less of the other. The iceberg is a lot bigger under the surface.

"No matter where I go, people say, 'You coach Chad Johnson.' He doesn't have to worry about people not knowing who he is. He doesn't have to draw attention to himself. Let's focus all our energy on playing better and respecting the game."

And that's why Marvin Lewis answers his phone at 3 a.m.

$\mathcal{B}$y December, the thermostat in Chad Johnson's Walnut Hills condominium is set at 85 degrees, eighty-five being his uniform number. Johnson claims to love the cold weather. Having grown up in south Florida and southern California, that's a little hard to believe, especially when it's hot enough in his living room to house a family of iguanas.

He has agreed to meet to discuss this book every Tuesday morning at 8, during the 2005 season. It's an ungodly hour for a pro athlete, whose internal clock hums best between noon and midnight. Johnson is almost always up and ready to talk. Something soft and soothing flows syrupy from his stereo: Frank Sinatra, Tony Bennett, Carlos Santana.

Unlike most of his peers, Johnson is not a one-note pony, beholden to hip-hop. When it comes to music, he is a Renaissance Man. There are days in the fall when he is the first player to arrive in

the Bengals dressing room at Paul Brown Stadium, just so he can put Bennett on the room's sound system.

He likes all music. His collection even includes musicals. When he lived in Los Angeles, Johnson saw stage versions of *Chicago* and *Moulin Rouge*. "They got me hooked," he says. "The singing. And man, the dancing." When you see him on a Tuesday morning in the fall, shades drawn, watching *West Side Story*, you begin to understand how Johnson might think that celebrating a touchdown by mimicking a scene from Riverdance would be a very cool thing to do.

He likes rap. Luther Campbell, the front man for the group 2 Live Crew and a founding father of the Liberty City Optimists football program, is a personal friend. Johnson is acquainted, too, with Trick Daddy, another Miami rapper. Rappers and athletes often run in the same circles. Especially in a place like Miami, where club-loaded South Beach is an international destination for the young rich and famous.

But Johnson likes Al Green, too, especially Green's gospel tunes. He listens to the rock group Blink-182. He enjoys Duke Ellington. Each Tuesday during the season, his first order of business is a trip to the drive-thru at the McDonald's on McMillan; after that, he visits F.Y.E., the music and video store, to scout new releases and old standards he figures he needs to expand his own tastes. One week, he buys Santana's classic album, *Abraxas*. The next, Ellington and Benny Goodman. In between, the newest movies to come out on video.

You would not think a 28-year-old star athlete, raised in the age of iPods and cable television, would be the least bit curious about Benny Goodman's clarinet playing. Think again. Misperceptions abound about professional athletes, fueled by a media concerned as much with personas as with sport. Athletes are rarely who they seem to be. The same week that former Atlanta Falcons safety Eugene Robinson was named NFL Man of the Year for his charity work, Miami police arrested him for soliciting a prostitute the night before his team was to play in the Super Bowl.

"I will never let the money and fame go to my head. My circle is the same as when I was catching the bus."

We think we know our heroes. Who we know is the image they choose to project. Chad Johnson is no different.

Image: Flashy, hyperactive, talkative to the point of distraction.

Reality: Not usually.

"He's very quiet," says Paula Johnson, his mother. The list of those Johnson trusts with his true feelings wouldn't fill up the inside of a matchbook.

Image: Laughing, joking life of the party.

Reality: Asleep by halftime of Monday Night Football.

Says Hue Jackson, Bengals receivers coach and one of Johnson's few confidantes, "Chad doesn't drink or smoke. He's not a guy that has to be out among the celebrities. I don't lose sleep on Saturday nights, worrying about Chad Johnson."

Johnson calls Jackson a lot, often at strange hours; the coach reciprocates.

"Where you at?" Jackson might ask, at midnight on a weeknight.

"Home."

"What you doing?"

"Chillin'."

Johnson does have his excesses: A fleet of twelve vehicles, a weakness for large pieces of expensive jewelry. Says his mother, "When he was 6, he'd be wearing my stepfather's rings. He has always loved jewelry."

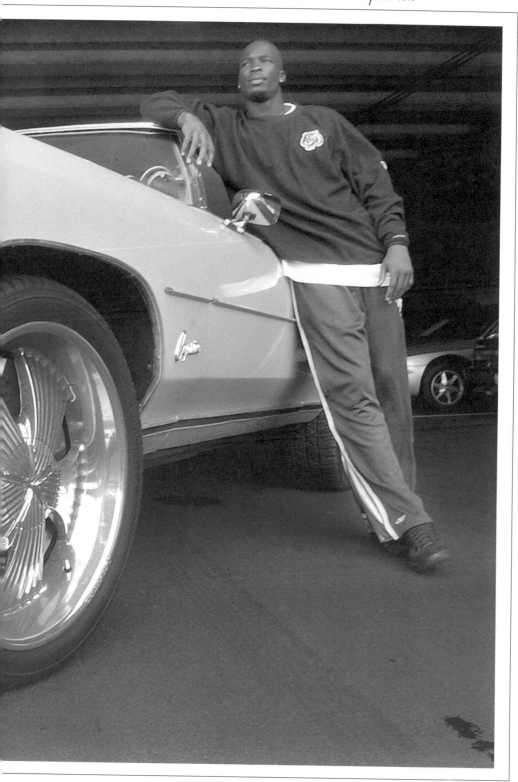

"Chad likes the simple things. All he wants is to have some Crystal Light in the fridge, his cell phone, his PlayStation and a McDonald's close by," Jackson says.

Image: Lots of friends, never without someone to talk to.

Reality: Acquaintance to many, close friend to very few.

Image: Egocentric star, football diva, requires pampering.

Reality: People person, craves attention almost as much as touchdown catches, stays regular.

Says Paula Johnson, "He looks at people one way. He's very trusting. There are no bad guys to him." Adds Chad, "I'm very humble outside of football. I'm as grounded a successful person as there is. I'm as cool as a window fan."

Image: It's all about me.

Reality: Not even close.

This is where the I Can't Be Stopped creation strays furthest from reality. You can put Johnson's name in the hatful of preening NFL wide receivers, whose end zone celebrations are as choreographed as any pass pattern they might run. From Billy "White Shoes" Johnson to Michael Irvin to Terrell Owens, wide receivers are the drama kings of the NFL. For originality, creativity, and sheer audacity, Johnson tops them all.

But it's not who he is. It's simply the most obvious and demonstrative manifestation of the joy he takes from playing football. "That's just him having fun," Paula says.

Twice last fall, the weeks of the Houston and Indianapolis games, Johnson paid for thirty of his friends and family to stay at a downtown Cincinnati hotel for three nights. He paid to fly them all in. "All the people I knew growing up," Johnson explains. "Same people I'm with in the off-season now."

He caters a soul food dinner on Friday night: Chicken, candied yams, greens, macaroni and cheese. Johnson does this every year.

Athletes enjoy saying they don't forget who they are and where they come from. In the sports vernacular, it is called "keeping it real."

Some do; most don't. The money and the fame spins their heads and their worlds. They land elsewhere and never look back. Johnson isn't that way. He owns a new, ten-bedroom home in Davie, Florida, an hour or so north of his grandmother's comfortable yet small home in Liberty City, where he grew up. The mansion was nearly complete early in 2006. Johnson chose to live in Liberty City, at his grandmother's. He stayed in the bedroom he slept in as a child. Hers was the only carport in the neighborhood that sheltered a Lamborghini.

"Nothing's changed," says Johnson. "Nothing will. I will never let the money and fame go to my head. My circle is the same as when I was catching the bus. It can all be taken away from me, easily. I could be back down in Liberty City tomorrow, with all those guys. I'm no better than they are. I'm just blessed."

Bessie Mae Flowers, his grandmother, raised Johnson in the church. He hasn't forgotten that, either. He's a member of the New Birth Baptist Church, in Opa-Locka, Florida. During games, Johnson has been known to recite to himself Philippians 4:13: *I can do all things through Christ who strengthens me.*

The image of star athletes clubbing until dawn, breezing past patrons waiting in line, to be seated in VIP sections where the liquor is free-flowing (and often free), is far from the truth. For six months, between July and January, NFL players lead cloistered, regimented lives. Those who don't generally aren't NFL players for long.

Five days a week, they spend ten or more hours a day in practice or meetings or getting treatment for various aches. They watch film. The sixth day, they play a game. Some might cut loose on Sunday night, after a home game. But not nearly as many as you might think. The money is too great—and the competition too fierce—for a smart player to blow his career at a club or on a barstool.

In Cincinnati, Chad Johnson does less partying than the average third-year law student. He goes to the stadium, he comes home. His condo is comfortable, but not large. It's strictly a place to sleep and relax. The refrigerator is nearly always empty, save for juice or sports drinks. The living room is what you'd expect to see in a middle-class home. It's just big enough for a sectional couch and a big-screen TV. The walls are decorated with four paintings of Johnson, in action.

Image: Chad Johnson must be a party animal.

Reality: During football season, he's as exciting as a game of Scrabble.

"My focus is strictly on football when I'm here, so the lack of things to do really doesn't matter," Johnson says. "When I'm home (in Miami) and off, I'm looking for things to get into. Down there, South Beach, everything's open until 6 in the morning. There's none of that here. That's perfect. I'm not here to be in the clubs."

You will not find Johnson's name on some Internet rumor board. You will not see him mentioned in a chat room or on a fans' website, at least not in connection with indulging in the local night life. He understands the pitfalls and temptations in being young, famous, and wealthy. Last season, he tried to share the knowledge with Bengals rookie wide receiver Chris Henry.

"I can teach him how to work, how to study film, and know his opponent on the field," says Johnson. "I can help him with running good routes. Life off the field is common sense. Be careful. Now that you've made it, your life is under a microscope.

When Johnson was a Bengals rookie, his veteran teammates nicknamed him "The Golden Child" because of the choppers.

It's such a small time in your life to be messing it up." Henry might have heard Johnson's advice. He didn't listen to it. Police cited Henry three times last offseason. Once in northern Kentucky during the season; after the year, in Orlando; then in Clermont County in June.

Johnson does have his excesses: A fleet of twelve vehicles, a weakness for large pieces of expensive jewelry. Says his mother, "When he was 6, he'd be wearing my stepfather's rings. He has always loved jewelry." And, of course, the gold-capped teeth. Johnson has had gold caps at least since he arrived at Santa Monica College. When Johnson was a Bengals rookie, his veteran teammates nicknamed him "The Golden Child" because of the choppers. No one close to him is a big fan of the teeth.

As Paula Johnson says, "My mother and I have hidden so many

pairs of those teeth. He just goes out and gets more. I've given up on that. He has to ask himself, is this the image he wants to portray?"

Johnson hates Tuesdays in the fall. It's the players' traditional off day during the season. Most players look forward to Tuesday, to sleep in, heal up and get away from the all-encompassing football grind. Not Johnson. He lives for the grind. It's football. No one loves the game more than he does.

He will eat his fast food and look for his music. He will run an errand. It's all just killing time, until he can go to Paul Brown Stadium on Tuesday afternoon, to pick up the DVDs of the next opponent's defense. On Tuesday nights, Johnson isn't at home, chillin'. He's at the stadium, pestering the Bengals coaches while they install the game plan.

"He's here almost every Tuesday night," said Bengals head coach Marvin Lewis. "I don't think he has missed a night, though there are some Tuesdays he really doesn't want to see me."

In 2005, several Bengals players began showing up in the coaches' offices on Tuesday nights. It was an atmosphere that Lewis had hoped to cultivate from the day he arrived. It speaks well of a team when its players care enough to come to work on their off day, whether it's to work out, hang out or take an active interest in the game plan.

Before 2005, it was unheard of for a Cincinnati Bengal to spend any more time on the job than was required. Any Cincinnati Bengal but Chad Johnson, whose best friend is football.

"He has been the instigator" of the Tuesday night sessions, said Lewis. The coach ticked off names of other regular attendees: wide receivers T.J. Houshmandzadeh and Tab Perry, linebacker Odell Thurman, several linemen. "When you have people who want to work, who actually look forward to it, that's when you're taking steps to be great," Lewis said. "That was a development (in 2005). But Chad has always come."

"Got to," Johnson says, simply. "If you want to be the best, you have to work like the best."

To that end, Johnson craved the ear of fellow wideout Jerry Rice. Rice, arguably the best to ever play the position, was playing for the Oakland Raiders in 2003 when the Bengals visited in the season's second week. Johnson tried to get Rice's attention at halftime, as the teams trotted off the field.

When that didn't work, after the game Johnson corraled a Raider named Justin Fargas, and asked Fargas if he would get a message to Rice. Johnson wanted tips on how to train in the off-season; Rice's workouts were grueling and legendary. Johnson asked Fargas to see if Rice would come back out onto the field. Johnson waited, long enough to miss Marvin Lewis' post-game message. Rice never came out.

Last fall, he went out before the Bengals home game with the Green Bay Packers. Normally, Johnson and Cincinnati quarterback Carson Palmer are on the field at 10:20, "doing the route tree," Johnson calls it. Wide receiver and quarterback run each pass play in the game plan, from both sides of the ball.

The day of the Green Bay game, instead of going into the Bengals dressing room after he'd finished with Palmer, for two ten-minute sessions in the hot and cold tubs, Johnson stayed on the field. He asked Packers quarterback and future Hall of Famer Brett Favre to throw him a pass. "I just wanted to catch a ball from him," Johnson said.

Marvin Lewis also credits Johnson with breaking down barriers between Bengals coaches and players. For years, the gulf between players and management was insurmountable. Players believed ownership didn't want to win; ownership didn't do anything to change that perception. Many former Bengals have said they went their entire careers in Cincinnati without speaking to owner Mike Brown.

That sort of us-versus-them atmosphere filtered down to coaches and players. Coaches before Marvin Lewis were seen by players as too close to ownership to be trusted. Not to Chad Johnson. Who, as his mother Paula says, trusts everyone.

Says Lewis, "Chad has broken down the barrier between players and coaches. He is helping us turn the corner that way. He knows we're all in this together." Lewis says Johnson was the first Bengal to ride on the first team bus to the stadium on game days. Traditionally, the first bus is reserved for coaches and front office staff. Not anymore. "There is no class system with him. No wall of separation," says Lewis.

"I have everybody on the same level. Nobody's better or worse in my book. I don't think there's another player in the league who gets along with his entire team the way I do," Johnson says.

He recalls his days in California, working menial jobs between junior college seasons. He appreciates what he has now. Johnson's former teammate at Santa Monica College, Carolina Panthers star wideout Steve Smith, pays tribute to his Keep It Real side by visiting the suburban Los Angeles Taco Bell where he worked, to keep himself humble.

Chad Johnson, who while living in L.A. worked as a stock boy at a toy store and in a men's clothing store, has his own way of keeping it real. When he's at a restaurant, he asks for a job application. It can be a fast-food place or a pizza joint. Johnson will fill out the application and turn it in. There are restaurants in Cincinnati now where a framed Chad Johnson job application hangs on a wall.

A few years ago, Johnson even spent a few Thursday nights during the season waiting tables at the LaRosa's pizza restaurant

One might spot Chad most anywhere, including playing pick-up basketball at Fifth Third
Arena on the University of Cincinnati campus, where he has also been known to turn
up as a "guest lecturer."

on North Bend Road on the west side of Cincinnati.

He has spent off days playing pick-up basketball at Fifth Third Arena on the University of Cincinnati campus. Johnson claims he could beat in one-on-one any member of the '04 Bearcats but forward Jason Maxiell. Maxiell went on to be a first-round draft pick of the Detroit Pistons of the National Basketball Association. Johnson's assertion drew laughs from then-senior UC players Armein Kirkland and Eric Hicks. "Chad could never even get a shot off against me," Hicks maintained.

Johnson has also spent a Tuesday afternoon in a UC classroom, as a "guest lecturer" in an advanced reporting class. He has been spotted at LaSalle and Elder high schools on Friday nights, watching football games. Why LaSalle and Elder? "They're the only two schools I know how to get to," Johnson says.

And so on. Athletes are not who they seem to be. Chad Johnson is no different. He is everything you might believe him to be. But not always. And never for long. The player you see dancing in the end zone on Sunday afternoon is often asleep by 10 Monday night. The gregarious sort you see on TV has no close friends in town. He needs people around him. But he doesn't let them get too close. "What you see is what you get," Johnson says, "unless you're Mom or Grandmom."

All that clubbing he does in Miami in the off-season? You could just as easily find him speaking to school kids, attending a Miami Heat basketball game, or hanging out at his grandmother's house. One day in January 2006, an especially perfect south Florida day, temperature in the mid-70s, not a cloud to intrude, Chad Johnson was in his grandmother's house, watching the NFL Network on TV. The league's draft "combine" was coming to him live from Indianapolis. The combine is the NFL's annual meat market for prospective pros. Johnson was checking out the Miami-born players.

It's all about the football. Even when it's not.

He needs people around him. But he doesn't let them get too close. "What you see is what you get," Johnson says, "unless you're Mom or Grandmom."

THE LOST DECADE

*C*had Johnson has sat in the Cincinnati Bengals "war room" on Draft Day, listening intently as the club decided whom to take with its first pick. It's not unusual for a player to be in the room with coaches and front office people the day of the draft; it's practically unheard of. But that's what Johnson does. He was 14 years old on April 26, 1992, when the Bengals took University of Houston quarterback David Klingler. If Johnson had been in the room for that one, he'd have fallen out of his chair.

It is patently unfair to saddle David Klingler with the ignominy of being the symbol of Bengals futility between 1992 and 2002, known most familiarly

in Cincinnati as The Lost Decade. It isn't right that Klingler should be seen as the captain of Cincinnati's ship of fools when, across those ten-plus-one miserable years, he had so much company. Standing shoulder to shoulder with the likes of owner Mike Brown, coach Dave Shula, and fellow QB Akili Smith (not to mention the ten other quarterbacks who made starts during that time), Dave Klingler isn't even in the center of the photo. If he were the captain, the ship hosted every admiral in the fleet.

And yet as a symbol of Bengals futility Klingler, bless him, stands the test of time. His legacy endures as a tragicomic testament to All Things Bengal. Which, during those unfortunate seasons, meant buffoonery.

"Where do we go now? We know where we're going. We're going down the drain."

Klingler was the starting quarterback for much of the 1993 season, at least in the games when he could walk. And '93 remains, arguably, the worst season in Bengals history. Which, by extension, makes it among the worst by one franchise in the history of the modern-era National Football League. At the very least, the '93 season established a benchmark for Bengals tomfoolery. It set the table for how things would be in Cincinnati until Marvin Lewis' arrival in 2003. It was emblematic of the sort of situation Chad Johnson walked into in 2001, his head filled with seemingly ludicrous visions of optimism and hope.

You could blame the 3-13 season of 1991, Sam Wyche's last as Cincinnati's head coach, on the rapid decline of several key veteran players and the front office transition following the death in August of team founder Paul Brown. You could look at the 5-11 year of 1992 and see a little progress.

144

By '93, no one was wearing blinders. The Lost Decade was in full throttle.

It is impossible, in one chapter of a book, to detail the gaffes and missteps the Bengals made during The Lost Decade. It is a book in itself, covered not in cloth, but in a brown paper sack. There is no way, in one brief burst of words, to describe adequately the misery of the players, the frustration of the fans and the abject incompetence of management. Suffice to say what started as pain eventually turned to laughter, once the coping skills kicked in. In football, as in most things, we have choices in the way we react to events in our lives. It is always better to laugh than to cry.

It started on Draft Day 1992. Conventional wisdom was that Cincinnati would take a defensive player with its first choice, the sixth overall in Round One. The Bengals defense had allowed 435 points the previous year, an average of more than 27 points a game. Opposing quarterbacks completed 60 percent of their passes against Cincinnati, and threw for nearly 250 yards a game. The pre-draft speculators figured the Bengals would take a defensive back, most likely Troy Vincent of Wisconsin.

David Klingler was with his agent, Leigh Steinberg, when the pick was announced. They were on TV. You could see Klingler's face register a mix of incredulity and pain. The TV audio picked up Steinberg's reaction: "Oh, boy. Mike Brown."

Two days later, from a charity golf tournament in Houston that Klingler was also attending, Cincinnati's incumbent/lame duck quarterback Boomer Esiason sized up the situation. Esiason said Klingler and Steinberg were "a little befuddled and probably not very happy about coming here."

Other Bengals were equally befuddled. "What are we doing?" asked safety David Fulcher. "I guess I assumed like everyone else that we would get some help on defense." Said wideout Tim

McGee, "Our two biggest strengths are quarterback and wide receiver. (Cincinnati's second pick was University of Tennessee wideout Carl Pickens.) So I guess we have depth now."

Bengals owner Mike Brown sized up his selection of Dave Klingler this way: "Who is the guy you would least like to play against the next ten years? When you get a quarterback with that good of talent, you'd better snap him up, because you might not get that chance for the next decade."

Coach Dave Shula, 32 years old and also in his first season, added his approval and expertise: "It has been my experience that having the quarterback position solidified gives you an opportunity to win championships."

Team brass saw Klingler's ability to run (4.7 seconds in the 40-yard dash), jump (25 feet in the long jump, 6 feet, 9 inches in the high jump) and lift (325 pounds in the bench press) and decided they had an athlete at QB. They likened Klingler's athleticism to that of tackle Anthony Munoz, a future Hall of Famer. They said his passes accelerated like Joe Namath's.

By the time he left the Bengals after the '95 season, Dave Klingler had started 24 games and lost 20 of them. He'd thrown 21 interceptions and 16 touchdown passes and been sacked so many times, his body was in permanent need of touch-up. By October 1994, an anonymous Bengals assistant coach was telling *The New York Times*, "It's obvious Klingler can't get it done."

Klingler's aloof nature didn't endear him to his teammates. By his last season, Klingler would sometimes eat his lunch in his truck, parked in the lot of the team's practice facility. The Bengals' selection of Klingler as their first pick in '92 was horrific, even by their standards.

Between '92 and '02, the Bengals had a top-ten pick in the first round a staggering nine times. Among players chosen with those picks were: Klingler, John Copeland, Dan Wilkinson, Ki-Jana Carter, Akili Smith, and Peter Warrick. Cincinnati's troubles might have started with poor drafting decisions. That was only the beginning.

Klingler missed nearly all of the '92 preseason because of a contract dispute. On the first snap from center in his first practice, he started to fade back and fell down. Metaphors get no better than that.

The Bengals lost their '93 opener, 27-14 to the Cleveland Browns. Dave Klingler was sacked six times and knocked down on five other occasions. It would soon become evident that the team had drafted a quarterback with no plans to protect him.

It only took three games, all losses, for the *Cincinnati Post* to proclaim in a September 22 headline, "1993 Bengals Could Challenge Worst Years in Franchise History." Players were grumbling. "Somebody has to step up and take control of this team," decided Carl Pickens, a thinly-veiled indictment of Shula.

The Bengals slipped to 0-4, with a 19-10 loss to the Seattle Seahawks. Klingler missed the second half after suffering a mild concussion. He returned two weeks later, to be sacked four more times in a 28-17 loss to Cleveland.

And so on.

At 0-7, Mike Brown offered the first of many threats to move the team, if a new stadium were not built. At 0-8, Jay Schroeder had assumed the quarterback duties, a move that prompted Klingler to suggest, "Clark Kent could play quarterback and it wouldn't make a difference. If (Shula) puts Jay out there, I'll be rooting for Jay, and if he puts me out there, then Jay better be ready."

Shula benched running back Harold Green. Because nobody had taken Carl Pickens' advice, players were saying whatever they felt, no matter who they might offend or disrespect.

"I guess Dave was quoted after the game as saying we're the worst team in Bengals history," Green said. "But for one, I think it may be touching a little close to home as him being the worst coach in Bengals history. Where do we go now? We know where we're going. We're going down the drain."

The Bengals lost their first ten games, then dropped to 1-12 with a comical 7-2 loss to the 1-11 New England Patriots. NFL commissioner Paul Tagliabue went to bat for Mike Brown, telling Cincinnati media how important it was to the future of the team to have a new publicly-funded stadium. Timing might have been of the essence. On this occasion, it wasn't the commissioner's strength.

The Bengals won two of their last three in '93, to finish 3-13. They followed that up with a bookend performance in '94. Shula's assessment of his team following the '94 season? The Bengals played well enough "to make the games exciting."

Fans hoping for major coaching and personnel changes were told that special teams coach Marv Braden had been fired. Immediately after the last game of the second consecutive 3-13 season, Mike Brown had his media relations staff handing out a press release in the locker room, announcing ticket price increases for the following year.

In '95, the Bengals traded up in the draft to take Penn State running back Ki-Jana Carter with the first overall pick. Carter agreed to a rookie-record $7.125 million signing bonus. In his third carry of the first preseason game, Carter tore the anterior cruciate ligament in his left knee. He went on to break his wrist in the '98 opener and miss thirteen games the following year because of a ruptured cyst in his right knee.

Carter gained 747 yards in his star-crossed five years as a

Bengal. He is remembered most for buying his teammates extra-large towels for use in the locker room. The team had always issued small, high school gym towels to its players. Comedy was watching 6-foot-5, 320-pound tackle Willie Anderson after a shower, trying to dry himself with a towel the size of a cereal box.

The Bengals released Ki-Jana Carter June 1, 2001.

The '96 season marked the end of the Dave Shula Era. The Bengals blew a 21-0 lead at San Francisco, dropping to 1-6 with the 28-21 loss. Shula finished with a 19-52 record, and a psyche so shattered he left coaching to run his father's chain of steak houses.

After the '94 season, veteran offensive lineman Bruce Kozerski had offered Shula a lifeline. "On the first day of (mini)camp (in May of '95) Dave has to let (players) know he holds the trump card for their career. Dave figures these guys are pros and that you shouldn't have to put your foot down. I think he has been taken advantage of a little bit."

Shula, like David Klingler, was in over his head. The quarterback was quiet, religious and prone to self examination. He never seemed to know how an NFL signal-caller should act. Klingler wasn't everything his predecessor Boomer Esiason was.

Klingler tried fist-pumping during games, a melodramatic expression of enthusiasm that rang hollow. He moved his locker next to his offensive linemen, an Esiason-esque move that backfired once he started complaining publicly about their performance. That was before an aging and substandard offensive line left his psyche broken and his body limp.

Ironically, Klingler's noble decision to stay at Houston his senior year might have hastened his pro demise. The Cougars were 10-1 Klingler's junior year, when he threw for 5,140 yards and 51 touchdown passes. They operated a run-and-shoot attack that featured Klingler's athleticism and preyed on a weak schedule.

Klingler finished fifth in the Heisman Trophy race, yet some saw him as the Number One overall pick in the draft, had he chosen to declare himself eligible.

As it was, he stayed at Houston, where a porous offensive line and a more difficult schedule his senior year took a toll on his numbers. The Bengals still believed him worthy of a high first-round choice, though, even if no other teams did.

Dave Shula, meanwhile, was the classic example of the pro sports adage that if you treat your players like men, they'll show you why you shouldn't. The Bengals hired Shula when he was 32, an age when most coaches in the NFL are still learning how to operate a videotape machine. Shula's NFL experience was limited to one year as Cincinnati's wide receivers coach and one as the quarterbacks coach with the Dallas Cowboys, where Pro Bowler Troy Aikman made fun of him behind his back. Not exactly the fast-track to a head coaching job, for any assistant not named Shula.

Bengals players didn't take Shula seriously. After awhile, it got worse than that. Tim Krumrie, the highly respected nose tackle, started calling Shula "the Boy Scout." When Shula asked players for their private phone numbers, Boomer Esiason gave him the main number for a Cincinnati pizza chain. In '92, Shula's first year, an aging veteran named Gary Reasons, signed to bolster the Bengals' thin linebacking corps, twisted Shula's ballcap around during a game. The move was caught on television.

In most NFL outposts, such blatant insubordination would have meant a suspension for Reasons, or worse. In Cincinnati, nothing happened. Ultimately, Dave Shula could not command his players' respect. Team owner Mike Brown restricted Shula's ability to make personnel moves, further hurting the coach's authority. By the time he was fired, Shula's post-game postmortems were

Chad Johnson was 14 years old in 1992, when Mike Brown drafted quarterback David Klingler. If Johnson had been in the room, he'd have fallen out of his chair.

painful to watch, often nothing more than a recitation of the injury report from the game.

"We're only one game out of first place," was a typical Shula remark, that one made after his team dropped to 1-3 to start 1996.

Both Shula and Klingler might have survived, had they been supported strongly on the field, on the sidelines, and by the owner. A franchise with a strong organization might have been able to see them through. As it was, there wasn't a worse organization in the entire NFL. Coach and QB could not have landed in a more difficult situation.

The Bengals had brief flares of hope during the Lost Decade: Jeff Blake's debut in 1995, Boomer Esiason's five-game swan song to close out the '97 season, and Bruce Coslet's 7-2 finish as interim coach after Shula's dismissal. Yet history kept repeating itself, in the same ways. The Lost Decade became Groundhog Decade.

Coslet came in spewing fire—"I'll be different," he said—yet he discovered what Shula knew, and Dick LeBeau would learn. Fire without authority is doused soon enough. Without the hammer of releasing people, the head coach didn't scare his players. The Bengals' lack of player leadership didn't help. After Esiason left for the safety of Monday Night Football broadcasts, Coslet had no lieutenants in the locker room. Who would he call on?

His best players were running back Corey Dillon and wide receiver Carl Pickens. The former was a Me-Firster with disturbing mood swings; the latter was universally regarded as a locker room tumor. Pickens' blatant ripping of Coslet got so bad, the Bengals in 2000 inserted a clause in player contracts that forbid public criticism. The penalty was the forfeiture of signing bonus money. It was known as The Pickens Clause.

Not that what Dillon and Pickens had to say was entirely without merit. When Dillon decided in 2000 that he'd "rather

Corey Dillon was the running back of The Lost Decade, then found himself in New England. Chad wanted to find himself in Cincinnati.

flip burgers" than play for the Bengals, he had a point. Meanwhile, Coslet's hand-picked quarterback, Jeff Blake, took all praise and accepted no blame and said he believed leadership was "overrated."

The bad drafts continued unabated, caused partly by the club's thin scouting department. Akili Smith was taken third overall in the '99 draft. By June 2000, Coslet was calling Smith "the real deal." Darnay Scott, the Bengals' best receiver, broke his leg in August. Smith started the opener at home against Cleveland, the first game at Paul Brown Stadium, and was awful, completing just 15 of 43 passes and throwing two interceptions in a 24-7 loss.

Five months earlier, in minicamp, players believed the new stadium would signal a new era. They were thrilled the club was dispensing ballcaps. And big towels. It says much about how the Bengals organization had treated its players over the years that the players would get truly excited over a free baseball hat.

"Four years here, I never got a hat," marveled a tight end named Marco Battaglia. "Now all I've got to do is hold out my hand."

The gushing praise over trinkets and bare necessities was too much for one Bengals fan. Ken Lawson wrote this to the *Cincinnati Enquirer*: "I nearly fell over backwards the other day when everyone was so excited to report that Mike Brown bought new towels for the team. It would not surprise me to learn that each new towel had a Marriott tag."

The Bengals arrived in Baltimore in Week 3 of the 2000 season just in time to tank the game. They lost 37-0 to the eventual Super Bowl champion Ravens, whose defense was coached by one Marvin Lewis. Coslet quit after the game. After the 7-2 start in '96, Coslet lost 28 of the last 35 games he coached.

Dick LeBeau, Cincinnati's defensive coordinator, was named coach. "LeBeau brings team discipline" was the headline in the September 28 *Cincinnati Enquirer*. Three days later, the disciplined defensive tackle John Copeland said the Bengals were known as "the junior college of pro football."

The Bengals lost LeBeau's debut, 31-16, to Miami. Afterward, LeBeau praised the Bengals for not giving up. After they dropped to 0-5, tackle Willie Anderson told *USA Today*, "I'm 25 and I'm aging a lot. Every single day. It makes it hard to go out in public."

Akili Smith looked lost at quarterback, as if he'd never played the position. In a 23-6 loss to Dallas, he completed 10 of 25 passes, for 68 yards. Smith blamed his wide receivers, for not staying after practice for extra work.

On December 2, when the Bengals were 2-10, the *Enquirer* reported the team would be $16.3 million under the salary cap for the 2001 season, the most in the league. A fan started the website mikebrownsucks.com. Throughout the 2000 and 2001 seasons, Dick LeBeau continued to praise his team's effort. The notion of Trying Hard became something to hold onto, in the final, typical days of the Lost Decade. Trying hard became a virtue, rather than a requirement. LeBeau had his players' respect and affection, but not their fear. They didn't play for him, just as they hadn't played for Shula or Coslet. And LeBeau's quarterback miseries were every bit as bad.

From Klingler to Blake to Smith— with a helping of Jay Schroeder, Scott Mitchell, Neil O'Donnell and Gus Frerotte on the side—the Bengals had bungled a decade, with no hope in sight.

This is what Chad Johnson eagerly became a part of, in April 2001. "I'm going to let you know right now, it's not the same old Cincinnati," he said May 9 of that year.

Everyone laughed then.

Johnson's laughing now.

CELEBRATION

On Christmas morning 2005, Chad Johnson woke up in his grandmother's house in Liberty City and watched his children open gifts. He doesn't recall the presents he got. Nor does he especially care. For a man known best for his celebrations, the year's biggest day of celebration passed quietly, just the way he liked it.

"What did I get for Christmas?" he said several days later, just before the Bengals played the Kansas City Chiefs. "I woke up. I'm here to see another day. Christmas is for my kids." Besides, as the multi-millionaire explained, "What do you buy me? A thirteenth car?"

It only seems as if Chad Johnson has been choreographing himself in the end zone forever. It only appears he has been doing stand-up comedy against defensive backs since he understood he had a mouth and what it could do. Off the field,

Chad Johnson is mostly subdued. On the field, he is anything but. Nothing shows the distance between the public player and the private man more clearly than his celebrations.

"He's like me in that respect," explains his mother, Paula Johnson. "He's quiet, but he likes to have fun. Those celebrations are just him having fun. I don't think he does it for attention."

Says his mentor Charles Collins, "Chad is Superman on Sunday. The rest of the time, he's Clark Kent. Chad doesn't really know how to be a celebrity. That's what people put on him. I would never let him wear those gold teeth when he trained with me, but you have to let him be him in the games."

Celebrating and trash-talking are the same things to Johnson. Yet until the 2005 season, Johnson merely dabbled in the art of end zone entertainment. Most of his notoriety came from wearing his uniform improperly.

The NFL fined him for wearing orange shoes. It fined him for wearing from his waistband a towel that was deemed too long. It fined him for not tucking in his jersey and for wearing his socks improperly. Former Bengals All-Pro safety David Fulcher was the league's man in Cincinnati, when it came to enforcing the dress code. Fulcher had an easier time tackling fullbacks. Said Robert Taylor, Johnson's coach at Santa Monica College, "David told me following Chad around on Sundays was a full-time job."

"I know you didn't go to church," said Johnson. "But it's Sunday, so I'm going to bless you, anyway."

Late in the 2003 season, after he scored during the Bengals 41-38 win over the San Francisco 49ers, Johnson jogged to the back of the end zone and picked up a poster-sized, hand-scribbled

"I'm never going to be boring in the end zone," says Johnson. "Fans don't want to see that. People paying $3,000 a season ticket don't want to see me hand the ball to the official."—Chad Johnson

note and lifted it toward a TV camera. "Dear NFL Please Don't Fine Me AGAIN!!!!!" he'd written.

The NFL didn't find it amusing. The league office hit him up for $10,000 for that harmless, if smart-alecky, indiscretion. That hiked Johnson's fine total for the '03 season to $70,000.

The NFL is America's most popular sports show, sometimes in spite of itself. It has been branded the "No Fun League" for its nit-picky rules regarding what it deems sportsmanlike conduct, especially when it comes to end zone antics. Attempts to stifle Johnson's football personality haven't gone well. On the second play of the first home game of the Bengals 2005 season, Chad Johnson turned a play called Fly Right 78 into a 70-yard

He was fined for wearing orange shoes, a towel that was too long, and his socks improperly. Chad violated the dress code so often and so thoroughly, the NFL considered hiring him a wardrobe man.

touchdown catch from quarterback Carson Palmer. His victim on the play was Minnesota Vikings' cornerback Fred Smoot, a friend of Johnson's and a frequent Pro Bowler. Smoot was beaten clearly. He couldn't say he hadn't been warned.

"I'm going to bless you today," Johnson had informed Smoot before the game.

"What?"

"I know you didn't go to church," said Johnson. "But it's Sunday, so I'm going to bless you, anyway."

This is standard Johnson trash-speak. When he's not blessing defensive backs, he's asking them how much money they make and telling them they're going to earn it trying to cover him. He asks them if their shoes are tied. He reminds them he will be there all day. He calls himself "7-11" because he's open all night. The end zone celebrations are more creative than the yakking, but no more essential to who Johnson is, on the field.

"On the field, I want to show you how good 85 is. Period," says Johnson. He has been told forever by coaches that his talking makes things harder for everyone, including him. The day Johnson believes that is the day he trades his shoulder pads for a shuffleboard cue.

"I'm going to be pumped up, regardless. I use the talking to get my opponent pumped up." Johnson believes his talking inspires those who cover him to play their best. Then, when he still beats them, it stokes his own confidence. "I talk, you get mad, play as good as you can and I still beat you. Do you know what that does for my game?

"No one has stopped me yet. I can't be stopped.

No defense can stop me. No player. I will continue to talk, to make sure whoever is playing in front of me is at their highest level."

It's just a game, he says. Either you're ready or you're not, no matter what Johnson might say to you. If you're not good enough, you're not playing. That's your incentive, not some loudmouth on the other side of the ball.

"Something I say is going to put pressure on you to play better? My words are going to make the other team play better? C'mon, man," Johnson says. "You have a job to do, no matter what I say. Your skill level is what it is."

It's how they do it in Miami. From the time Johnson was a 4-year-old nose tackle who weighed less than fifty pounds, everybody talked. Coaches talked at other coaches, parents talked at coaches, players talked at parents. By the time they finally kicked the ball off, late in August, everyone connected with kids' football in Overtown or Liberty City knew what everyone else had said, about everything. Talking was as much a part of the game as playing.

"The coaches hated to lose," Johnson recalls. "They'd be screaming at us like we were grown folks. The way I grew up, everything was a competition. We had a passion for the game in Miami that was different from anywhere else."

At age 28, three times a Pro Bowler, Chad Johnson is still the same high school kid who tied classmates' shoes together, as they dozed in class. He's the same Chad who skipped class, hid from teachers, and showed up at Santa Monica games wearing lime-green suits with matching hats. He's the very little boy in his Sunday-best white suit, sitting in the redecorating dust of Bessie Mae Flowers' living room.

Only now, he's proposing to cheerleaders, dancing like an Irishman, and performing various bizarre acts on the football, such as putting it and, of course, giving it CPR. As Johnson's success has advanced, so has his end zone showmanship. Scoring a touchdown has become an appetizer for Johnson. It is the bread that gets the butter to the mouth.

"How much of it is entertainment? All of it," Johnson says. "I entertain. That's what I do. I am an athlete. That's a given. Now, I'm at the point where entertaining is what I love to do."

Much more than the trash-speak, which is largely private, man-on-man and out of the reach of microphones, the celebrating is what has earned Johnson whatever reputation he has. It's calculated, to be sure. As Craig Austin, his offensive coordinator at Santa Monica College, put it, "It's all marketing. He had those gold teeth when he played for us. He knew back then how to do things that would set him apart."

But there's more to it than brazen self promotion. It really is an eruption of unchained joy, from a person whose passion for football has always defined him. Says Hue Jackson, the Bengals wide receivers coach and arguably Johnson's closest acquaintance on the team, "Do I worry about his future, that he'll still think as a 50-year-old man he can run down the field and catch passes? Yes, I do."

On the field, what you see is what you get with Chad Johnson. There is no posing. Johnson's ego might be getting some serious gratification, but that's not his intent.

"He doesn't have that ego to him, you know?" says Jonathan Smith, Johnson's quarterback at Oregon State. "It's all fun with him."

And for those who cheer him. "I'm never going to be boring in the end zone," says Johnson. "Fans don't want to see that. People paying $3,000 a season ticket don't want to see me hand the ball to the official. They want to see my personality."

And there is this: When the Bengals drafted Johnson in April of 2001, he vowed to turn around the franchise's sorry fortunes, a guarantee more wishful than bold at the time. "I'm going to let you know right now," Johnson announced in May of that year. "It's not the same old Cincinnati."

The celebrating—the fun—was another sign that the Bengals would be turning the corner, with their talky, fun-loving wide receiver riding shotgun and directing traffic.

You don't celebrate when your team is terrible, lest you look selfish and foolish. Johnson didn't turn cheeky until the team turned watchable. And even then, he limited showtime to occasions the team was ahead. The celebrating isn't merely preening. It is another manifestation of a team doing exactly what Johnson said he would help it do.

How many years were the Bengals so bad, the only celebrating they did was to announce the end of the season? Was there a better manifestation of the "new" Bengals that Johnson had promised than the man himself having fun in the end zone?

Ickey Woods turned the 1988 Super Bowl season into a Shuffle party. No one ever accused him of showboating or self promoting. Everyone just wanted him to dance. The Shuffle assumed iconic status at Super Bowl XXIII, where team patriarch Paul Brown performed it during a press conference. (The NFL even tried to curtail Woods' harmless show, forcing him to dance behind the

Bengals bench, rather than in the end zone.)

There are those who believe, that given the pain involved in the profession, and the relatively short time its practitioners get to enjoy it, that celebrating should be encouraged, or at least endured. There are others, from the act-like-you've-been-there-before school, who think celebrating of any sort is a threat to the moral fiber of our nation.

Even those people liked The Riverdance.

September 25, 2005, Chicago: Johnson beat Bears cornerback Charles Tillman on a post pattern, for an 18-yard TD catch. He retreated to the back of the end zone and kicked his heels. A black man doing an Irish dance in a city made famous by an Italian gangster named Al Capone. What a wonderful world.

He'd seen the TV commercial, promoting the production of *Riverdance* at a Cincinnati amphitheatre called Riverbend. That was all it took. Johnson practiced it in the bathroom of the visitors' dressing room before the game. "I saw T.O. (his close friend Terrell Owens) do a Michael Jackson thing," Johnson recalled, the week after the dance. It was funny. But I knew I had to top it."

After that game, Johnson's cell phone message box was full. "Friends, Mom, coaches in Miami. The bishop at my church called. They were on the floor," Johnson said. (Johnson says even Bengals coaches get a kick out of his end zone act, usually while re-running his celebrations on videotape the following week. It's a claim head coach Marvin Lewis doesn't dispute.)

The *Cincinnati Enquirer*, in a special Bengals section leading up to the playoff game with the Pittsburgh Steelers, decided the Riverdance was Johnson's best effort of the season. It had heavy competition.

The array of celebrations Johnson offered in 2005 revealed a

Horsing around with his trusty steed, Bobbie Williams, who generally is carrying a much heavier load than the wide receiver.

man of surpassing depth, generosity, romance, and breeding. Not to mention chrome-soled size-11 Reeboks, "so when I beat guys, they have something shiny to look at."

Not since a New Orleans Saints receiver named Joe Horn pulled a cell phone from the goal post padding and pretended to make a call after he'd scored had an NFL player showed such wit upon finishing a touchdown. Any day now, Johnson's end zone displays will be reviewed in *The New Yorker*.

After he caught a 68-yard touchdown pass against Indianapolis

November 20, Johnson ran to the Bengals sideline and, on bended knee, mock-proposed to Bengals cheerleader Daphne Henrich. The bit had been prearranged. The previous Tuesday, Johnson had been watching film at Paul Brown Stadium when the notion struck. The Ben-Gals cheerleaders were practicing on the indoor basketball court inside PBS when Johnson asked them to take part.

"Whoever is on the end where I score, I'm going to pretend to propose," he said. "You have to react seriously." Henrich, a 30-year-old account executive for a Cincinnati radio station, wasn't prepared. She wasn't the closest cheerleader to Johnson, but she was the closest to the television cameramen he had summoned, while he was running into the end zone.

"He actually said, 'Will you marry me?'" Henrich recalled, months later. "I said, 'Of course I will.'" She was a media star for several days. People at ESPN2 initially believed Johnson's proposal was serious, and invited Henrich to appear on the network's program, "Cold Pizza."

"I don't think anybody can top that," Johnson said recently. Someone could.

On Christmas Eve, Johnson scored late in the first half against the Buffalo Bills, then looked around in dismay, because the cheerleaders already had retreated to the warmth of their dressing room. Johnson had asked them that morning to dance with him in a Rockettes-style chorus line.

Thwarted, Johnson jogged toward a large cloth bag he'd stashed behind the Bengals bench. It contained signed Johnson souvenirs. From behind the bench, Johnson fished out autographed ballcaps, footballs and T-shirts and tossed them to several fortunate fans seated in the first few rows.

Johnson set up the giveaway during the week. He claimed to have hit and injured a deer driving home from practice. He said the wounded animal was in his garage, and he would be bringing it to the game Sunday. Anyone who knew where Johnson lived— in Walnut Hills, near Eden Park—and the route he took home from Paul Brown Stadium would have recognized it was a prank.

As it was, some were not amused. One outraged Cincinnatian even called the SPCA. Somehow, the group reached Johnson by cell phone and wanted to know why he had an injured deer in his garage.

Johnson messed with Pittsburgh Steelers fans, wiping his mouth at lunchtime with a Terrible Towel. Then after the game, a 38-21 Bengals win at Heinz Field, he left a piece of the towel on the visiting locker room floor.

He's discriminating. Johnson had a square dance celebration ready to go in Nashville. He had a big day against the Titans—eight catches, 135 yards and a touchdown—but didn't do-si-do around the goal post because officials were huddling to discuss a penalty. "I can't use that one unless we're in Nashville," he said the following week.

He's multi-talented. After scoring in a 42-29 win against Baltimore, Johnson removed a pylon from the corner of the end zone, putted the football, then pumped his fist like Tiger Woods.

He's cautious. After the Tennessee game five weeks earlier, Johnson had asked a referee if he'd be penalized for picking up the pylon. "He told me, 'You're not supposed to use objects, but the pylon is a part of the field,'" Johnson said. "I figured they wouldn't throw a flag on me at a home game. And what else could I do with a pylon?"

Johnson doesn't even like golf. He thinks it's boring. Plus, as his Santa Monica teammate Eugene Sykes put it, "Chad's a perfectionist. If he can't do something great, he won't do it. Golf takes so much work."

CELEBRATIONS: *the ratings*

Keyshawn is more the talking type. I'm more of a keep my mouth shut. I lead by example on the field.—Chad Johnson, speaking of himself and his cousin, NFL wide receiver Keyshawn Johnson, on April 22, 2001, the day the Cincinnati Bengals drafted him in the second round.

Maybe it's a good thing Chad Johnson isn't always a leader on the field, lest the rest of his teammates begin proposing to cheerleaders, distributing Christmas gifts to fans seated behind the Bengals bench and giving CPR to the football. What would the National Football League make of that?

Ranking the celebrations:

1—*The Proposal, 11/20/05, vs. the Indianapolis Colts at Paul Brown Stadium.* Johnson scored on a 68-yard pass from Carson Palmer. As he neared the goal line, he motioned for a TV cameraman to follow him. Johnson trotted to the Bengals sideline, dropped to one knee and took the hand of Ben-Gals cheerleader Daphne Henrich, a 30-year-old account executive at a local radio station. "Will you marry me?" he asked Henrich. Johnson had told the cheerleaders earlier in the week to be ready, so Henrich wasn't entirely surprised.

2—*The Riverdance, 9/25/05 vs. the Bears in Chicago.* After catching an 18-yard TD pass from Palmer, Johnson did his best Irish imitation. Which, given that his only instruction came from watching a TV commercial for the production *Riverdance*, was impressively credible. Two months later, Pittsburgh Steelers wideout Hines Ward offered a lame imitation.

3—*Ho-ho-ho, 12/24/05, vs. the Buffalo Bills at PBS*. Johnson reached into a sack behind the Bengals bench after catching a 41-yard TD pass. He tossed signed shirts and ballcaps to fans seated behind the Bengals bench. The set-up was as good as the celebration: Earlier that week, Johnson claimed to have hit and injured a deer while driving home from practice. He said the animal was recuperating in his garage, and promised he would bring it with him on Sunday. The "reindeer" didn't exist. But that didn't stop local animal lovers from wondering publicly how Johnson could mistreat a deer that way.

4—*Tiger Chad, 11/27/05, vs. the Baltimore Ravens at PBS*. Even though he claimed to have cleared it with an official a few weeks earlier, the NFL fined Johnson $5,000 for removing an end zone pylon and pretending to putt the football with it. This is Ironic Chad: Johnson dislikes golf.

5—*CPR, 10/9/05, vs. the Jaguars in Jacksonville*. Chad scores on a 14-yard pass, then revives the football. The football made it; the Bengals didn't. Their 4-0 start was stopped, 23-20.

6—*Been There Before, 12/18/05, vs. the Lions in Detroit*. The high shock value of simply handing the official the ball after scoring could only be achieved by Johnson.

7—*No Chorus Line, 12/24/05, vs. the Bills at PBS*. The plan had been for Johnson and the Ben-Gals to dance in can-can, Rockettes fashion. But his TD grab came so late in the first half, the girls had already gone to their dressing room to get warm. That's when he played Santa.

8—*I'm Losing Money Here, 12/14/03, vs. the San Francisco 49ers, PBS*. Because of various violations of the league's dress code, Johnson was out of pocket tens of thousands of dollars. After scoring, he jogged to the back of the end zone, where he grabbed a posterboard sign on which he had printed, "Dear NFL Please Don't Fine Me AGAIN!!!!!" It cost him $10,000. Johnson paid $70,000 in fines during the 2003 season.

9—*Best Dance that Didn't Happen*: The Ickey Shuffle, which Johnson planned to do in the 2005 postseason. He had also considered the Ali Shuffle.

10—*The Pushups, 9/25/05, vs. the Bears in Chicago*. Watching Johnson attempt several push-ups after scoring his first touchdown against the Bears made you wonder how he made it to the NFL. He redeemed himself later, with the Riverdance.

"Everybody likes golf. Everybody but me," said Johnson. When reminded that golf is a game he can play until he's 70, Johnson thought for a minute. "So is PlayStation," he said.

He's fitness-conscious. Johnson did a few pushups after his second touchdown catch in Chicago.

He's a man you want in an emergency. On a Sunday night in Jacksonville, a national ESPN audience saw him administer CPR to the football.

"Scoring is the easy part," Johnson explained. "Coming up with new celebrations is hard."

One week, Johnson trotted off the field after he'd scored and had fellow wideout T.J. Houshmandzadeh drape a Bengals No. 81 jersey on his back. It was stitched with the name "Owens," a tribute to his friend Terrell, who had been suspended by the Philadelphia Eagles, a ruling upheld in arbitration. "I told him I was going to carry both of us on my back since he couldn't play," Johnson said. "It was just for a minute. I thought TV would see it, it was right after I scored."

Also that day, late in the 2005 regular season, Johnson said his good friend would be playing for the Dallas Cowboys in '06. "I should go get the jersey right now," he said. Four months later, Terrell Owens signed with Dallas.

Johnson refutes all comparisons to his friend Owens. Other than the celebrations, he says, their personalities could not be more different. "I never show anybody up. I'm into pleasing everybody. People watching, people coaching, players on my team. I don't want to let anybody down," said Johnson. "Everybody loves eighty-five."

Johnson might have always been the class clown. He wasn't always cutting up on the football field. In fact, until he reached the NFL, the field was generally the last place he acted out. "He didn't

The receiving team with the unlikely name of Johnson and Houshmandzadeh have
managed to carry over their prowess from Oregon and their college days.

celebrate with us because we didn't put up with that mess here,"
was how Robert Taylor, Johnson's junior college coach, put it.

He played a single season of big-time college ball, at Oregon
State. He arrived there late, because he had to take summer school
classes just to qualify to enroll. Johnson was so busy learning the
playbook and where to line up, he didn't have time to choreograph
his triumphs.

Were it not for quarterback Jonathan Smith and
Houshmandzadeh, his teammate on the Bengals and at Oregon
State, hand-signaling him as both lined up, Johnson would

Chad with his best girl—his daughter—who carries on the family tradition of good looks, which is found in Chad's mother, Paula, as well as her mother, Bessie Mae.

not have known where to stand on most plays. "He was a little more laid back, because he was learning," said Dennis Erickson, Johnson's coach at Oregon State.

In fact, Houshmandzadeh was far more demonstrative than Johnson at Oregon State. Jonathan Smith recalls the Beavers' home crowd yelling "Hooooosh" whenever T.J. made a big play. The one time Chad was Chad at OSU, it almost cost his team a touchdown. The Beavers were pounding Notre Dame in the Fiesta Bowl when Johnson hauled in a 74-yard touchdown pass from Smith. It was typical Johnson: He simply outran the defensive back. "The guy pulls up, like he has a groin injury," Jonathan Smith recalled years later. "But the truth was, Chad just beat him."

Johnson held the ball behind his head for the last several yards, then dropped it at the 1-yard line, believing he had crossed the goal line. "I was cruising," Johnson recalled five months after the game. "I knew I had left everybody. Toward the goal line I had seen a white line so I thought, OK, I'm already past the goal line, and I dropped the ball. I did not realize the end zone was painted all black."

Said Erickson, "He was 20 yards behind everybody and he was celebrating. I was pissed off, but fortunately the refs didn't see it."

Johnson has a few celebrations he didn't get to use. The (Muhammad) Ali Shuffle, for one. And the one he really regrets not being able to unwrap: His own version of the Ickey Shuffle. Johnson had given that one serious thought the week before the playoff game with Pittsburgh. "A dance of special significance," he'd called it.

Even Woods got into the act, volunteering his time to help Chad with the delicate footwork involved. But after halftime of that game, no Bengal was in a dancing mood, least of all Chad Johnson.

Maybe this year.

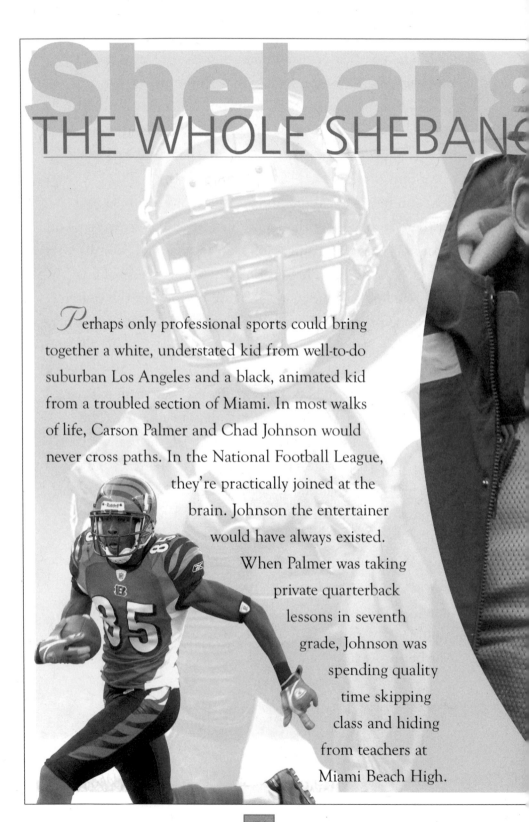

Shebang

THE WHOLE SHEBANG

*P*erhaps only professional sports could bring together a white, understated kid from well-to-do suburban Los Angeles and a black, animated kid from a troubled section of Miami. In most walks of life, Carson Palmer and Chad Johnson would never cross paths. In the National Football League, they're practically joined at the brain. Johnson the entertainer would have always existed. When Palmer was taking private quarterback lessons in seventh grade, Johnson was spending quality time skipping class and hiding from teachers at Miami Beach High.

But without Palmer's golden arm, the "golden child"—so named by his teammates as a rookie, for his gold-capped teeth—would not have dreams nearly so lofty, or attainable.

One needs the other. Each makes the other better. Both think about football the way spiders think about flies. It doesn't matter that Palmer drives a truck, Johnson a fleet of "pimped" rides, not the least of which is a '60s-vintage pink Chevrolet Caprice. Nor is it of consequence that Johnson likes to talk and Palmer likes not to.

"We're completely different. Outside of football, we don't have much in common," Johnson said.

Inside the game, they could be twin sons of different mothers, save for the celebrating. Palmer would rather be a regular in the *National Enquirer* than highlight himself the way Johnson does. Yet each in his own way is a football wonk. The difference is, Johnson will discuss his passion for the game, as well as display it openly on Sundays. Palmer lets his work speak for itself. It's the difference between a sunset and a fireworks display.

During the 2005 season, Johnson turned down an invitation to appear on David Letterman, because it would have interfered with his game preparation. (Johnson did make a mid-week appearance on HBO, with Bob Costas, but it was during the Cincinnati Bengals' bye week.)

"Run the route," says Palmer. "If you're open and you're where you're supposed to be, you'll get the ball."

When a reporter asked Palmer if he'd consider appearing on a late-night show, the quarterback looked at his inquisitor as if the man had an eye in the middle of his forehead. Ben Roethlisberger, the Pittsburgh Steelers quarterback, appeared with Letterman in 2004, during Roethlisberger's rookie year. It didn't sit well with Steelers coach Bill Cowher. Bengals coach Marvin Lewis would have no such worries with his two star offensive players.

Especially with Palmer. Considerate and polite to a fault, Palmer nevertheless can be as dry as winter hands. The presence his teammates on offense swear he has on the field is deliberately hidden in front of the media. Palmer offers very little of substance during interviews, beyond boilerplate praise of opponents and we'll-be-OK assessments of his own team. He has never revealed anything of himself beyond what is seen on the field.

A synergy exists between the best quarterbacks and their receivers that defines how successful they will become. At the highest level, passer and catcher know instinctively where the other will be, at any given moment. It requires the synchronicity of ballet and the intuition of a mind reader. There is no room for thinking, not when the average time a quarterback has to throw a pass in the NFL is less than four seconds. There is only time to react.

It started with Palmer and Johnson in the fall of 2004, when they made a trip to Indianapolis in Palmer's Chevy Silverado, to watch the Indianapolis Colts play the Minnesota Vikings on Monday Night Football. Specifically, to study Colts' quarterback Peyton Manning and his favorite target, Marvin Harrison. Manning and Harrison are the Astaire and Rogers of the NFL. Each is a Pro Bowl player and future Hall of Famer that thrives by knowing the other's intentions.

Palmer and Johnson came away from the experience knowing how far they had to go, but realizing it was achievable. "They're so good, all they have to do is look at each other," Johnson said of Manning and Harrison. "Manning knows the offense so well.

He knows there's a hole in every defense. He just checks the play at the line, toward the weakness of the coverage. We do the same thing, but Carson doesn't have the control Peyton has. Carson's right there. But it comes from experience and repetition.

"We're nowhere near those two, but we're good early. Carson didn't come in and have that bad first year like Peyton did." Indy went 1-15 in Manning's first season.

One play as much as any other during the 2005 season symbolized what Palmer and Johnson are striving for. It came in the Bengals' sixth game, in Nashville against the Tennessee Titans. The highly favored Bengals trailed 20-17 when Palmer completed a 15-yard touchdown pass to Johnson with 4:19 left in the game.

Most of the game, the Titans had defensed Johnson the way most teams do: They covered him at the line of scrimmage with a cornerback, then "rolled" a safety to Johnson's side of the field. Johnson works against double coverage nearly every week. On the touchdown, the Titans gambled and left cornerback PacMan Jones one on one with Johnson. Palmer recognized it, and quickly audibled to a slant-and-go pass to Johnson. The touchdown led the Bengals to a 31-23 win.

"Carson and I went on our own page," Johnson explained, a few days after the game. "It was one-on-one coverage. There aren't many situations where I'm going to have that."

When experts talk about Palmer's rapid ascent among NFL quarterbacks—he was a Pro Bowl player in only his second season as a starter—they mention most frequently his surprisingly advanced ability to read defenses, to grasp quickly what opposing teams are trying to do to stop the Bengals offense. His ability to get Johnson the ball so frequently—Johnson had a personal-best 97 receptions—even as the wide receiver was double-teamed is a testament to that.

"He should have laces in the back of his head," said Petros Papadakis,
a Southern Cal tailback between 1998 and 2000, about Carson Palmer.

Palmer also is the calm to Johnson's storm. Dylen Smith, Johnson's QB at Santa Monica College, would tame Chad's excesses by refusing to throw to him. Carson Palmer will politely tell Johnson to zip it. "Run the route," Palmer has been known to say. "If you're open and you're where you're supposed to be, you'll get the ball. Don't wave your arms, don't throw your hands up, don't cut the route short."

Keeping everyone happy in an offense as potent as Cincinnati's was in 2005 is a full-time job. A big part of Johnson's maturation as a player is understanding he doesn't have to catch 10 passes a game to be effective. And to keep a level head on days when the ball isn't coming his way. Jon Kitna, the former Bengals quarterback and one of Johnson's early mentors in the NFL, once told him his career would be defined two ways: By how he handled injuries and how he dealt with not getting the ball.

Given that Johnson hasn't missed a game since his rookie year of 2001, the injury question hasn't been an issue. The other is a work in progress. Johnson complained to Palmer during a Sunday night game in Jacksonville in October 2005 that he wasn't getting the ball enough. He went overboard with it at halftime of the playoff loss to Pittsburgh.

But in two other games, Johnson showed the maturity his coaches say he needs to be a great receiver. He had just two catches for 22 yards in Cincinnati's 23-20 win over Cleveland, yet he caused two penalties against Cleveland defensive backs in Cincinnati's game-winning drive, and made a crucial first-down catch on the same march.

The Browns' double teams of Johnson also freed running back Rudi Johnson to run for a season-high 169 yards. "Earlier in my career, I wouldn't have known how to react to being played that way," Johnson said. "It's bigger than just me now. We ran the ball

"He allows me to coach him," says Hue Jackson, and while he doesn't praise his prize pupil, there are plays he cannot help but celebrate.

because I'm taking two and three people out of the play. I did my job without catching the ball. I'm understanding that now."

During the game, Kitna reminded Johnson of what he had told him three years earlier, after the game at Indianapolis in which Johnson allowed a potentially game-tying touchdown catch bounce off his helmet:

"Man, I want to contribute," Johnson told Kitna.

"You are contributing," Kitna said. "By them doubling you, Rudi is averaging six yards a carry."

Earlier in the '05 season, the Houston Texans defense crossed up the Bengals. What Johnson and Palmer had seen on film was not what they saw during the game. Johnson came in licking his chops, expecting single coverage. What he got was double coverage most of the game. Johnson did catch seven balls, for just 67 yards. But teammate T.J. Houshmandzadeh had eight catches for 105 yards, the beneficiary of one-on-one coverage.

"I take satisfaction in that," said Johnson, several days after the game, a 16-10 Cincinnati win. "It's hard, though. I want the ball. It's never easy for me to stay patient. Move me around, let me make a play. But I know it's not going to happen every week."

What matters to those who see Johnson's potential—Marvin Lewis, Hue Jackson, Charles Collins—is that Johnson remains consistent and intent on getting better. That's not an issue for Palmer, who seemed born to play quarterback. Said Petros Papadakis, a Southern Cal tailback between 1998 and 2000, "He should have laces in the back of his head."

Papadakis said Palmer's passion for the position was such that in college, he was always looking for someone to throw to, or to watch film with. "I never pushed him," said Palmer's father Bill, a financial planner. "He was always pushing."

Bill Palmer moved from Los Angeles to Connecticut just as Carson was entering high school. The family stayed in L.A., believing Carson would see better competition and get more exposure there than on the East Coast. For four years, Bill Palmer spent weekends in an airplane, commuting to and from Connecticut and Los Angeles. He did not push his son into playing the game. He simply nurtured Carson's ability. "It just seemed reasonable," Bill Palmer said. "If he was a soccer player, I'd have sent him to soccer camp. Carson is gifted. We were able to develop it."

"I want the ball. It's never easy for me to stay patient."—Chad Johnson

While Palmer quietly took apart opposing defenses in 2005, Johnson reveled in the smack-talk spoils of victory. His favorite word that fall was "ridiculous." As in, "The options we have? It's ridiculous. Brat's up there pushing buttons and smoking cigars," Johnson said, in reference to offensive coordinator Bob Bratkowski, after only Cincinnati's second game, a 37-8 pounding of the Minnesota Vikings.

And again, after the opener, a 27-13 win at Cleveland: "Teams don't stand a chance with our offense. Wait 'til we're 7-0. If we're 7-0, I'll see you in Detroit," site of that year's Super Bowl. "Period. No question. We're going to win. You do not want to play this offense. You do not want to play us Week 17 or 18 with all the options we have. We'll be hitting on all cylinders then. Ridiculously."

Yet no pro sports season changes faces as often as an NFL season does. None has the potential for such dramatic change, week to week, depending on injuries and the whims of the schedule. The Bengals clinched their first division title in fifteen years by winning 11 of their first 14 games. Their offense could look, on occasion, just as Johnson described. Palmer led the league in touchdown passes. Rudi Johnson broke his own team record for rushing yards. T.J. Houshmandzadeh had a personal-best 78 catches. Chad Johnson did the same with 97 receptions and 1,432 yards.

But the Bengals lost their last three games, including the playoff defeat to Pittsburgh. Everyone, it seemed, needed to get better. "Once we got to the playoffs, I wanted it all," Chad Johnson said, after the 2005 season ended. "The whole shebang. I got greedy. You know how they say you got to crawl before you walk? This would have been like skipping the crawl and the walk and just taking off running. Just three more wins, that's all."

Johnson was characteristically candid about his own need to improve. As brash as he is about his ability—"I'm a Hall of Famer already," Johnson said, soon after the '05 season—Johnson is equally willing to admit he isn't the player he can be. "To get where I want to go, I have to do the same things year after year. Catching, blocking, running the right routes, being where I'm supposed to be. Even eating the right food and how I dress. I can always become a better pro."

The Pittsburgh loss deflated the whole city, but no one more than Johnson, whose desire to win is as deeply ingrained as his need to show the world how good a player he is. "The game would have been different had Carson not gone down" with a knee injury on Cincinnati's second offensive play, Johnson said. "Without Captain Kirk, Star Trek didn't work. I was crying once I saw the trainers come out. I knew it was bad.

"My main goal was getting us to the playoffs. My year was OK. But I should lead the league from now on. I should lead the NFL in catches and yards. The AFC is cool, but I've dominated the AFC for three years."

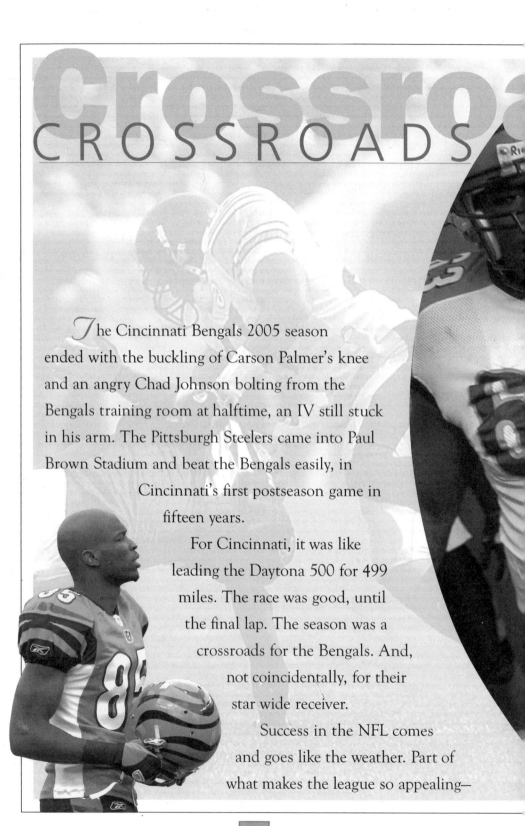

CROSSROADS

Crossroa

The Cincinnati Bengals 2005 season ended with the buckling of Carson Palmer's knee and an angry Chad Johnson bolting from the Bengals training room at halftime, an IV still stuck in his arm. The Pittsburgh Steelers came into Paul Brown Stadium and beat the Bengals easily, in Cincinnati's first postseason game in fifteen years.

For Cincinnati, it was like leading the Daytona 500 for 499 miles. The race was good, until the final lap. The season was a crossroads for the Bengals. And, not coincidentally, for their star wide receiver.

Success in the NFL comes and goes like the weather. Part of what makes the league so appealing—

the economics that ensure every team has the same money to spend and, theoretically, the same chance to win—also makes it difficult for teams to sustain success. In the last decade only the New England Patriots, winners of three of the previous five Super Bowls, have proven they can maintain superiority across several seasons.

After winning the AFC North division championship in '05, the Bengals are no different. Key players will be signed away by other teams. Crucial others will be lost to injury. Quarterback Carson Palmer tore two knee ligaments in the playoff loss to Pittsburgh. Can the Bengals build on the good they did in 2005? Can Chad Johnson?

Johnson has audacious goals. He wants to play past the age of 40. He knows Jerry Rice played until he was 42. He wants to have 1,800 receiving yards in a season. Only Rice has done that. He wants to be seen as the best receiver in Bengals history. And in the history of the NFL.

Said Hue Jackson, the Bengals wide receivers coach, "Money to Chad doesn't mean anything. What he perceives he is seen as is what matters."

"If I did it the right way, would I still be as hungry? Maybe that struggle was good."

"No matter what I accomplish, I'm still setting ridiculous goals," said Johnson. "Eighteen-hundred receiving yards is damned near impossible, because of the defensive schemes and the double coverage." And yet, as the halftime incident against Pittsburgh showed, Johnson's passion for the game can have mixed results.

What Johnson took from that, and what his mentors and

coaches hope he took from it, aren't exactly at odds. But they are different. Intellectually, Johnson understands he needs to harness his emotions in situations like that. Pro Bowl veterans' actions leave their marks on impressionable young players, good and bad. The Bengals locker room was tumorous through much of the 1990s, when their best players were also their most divisive.

Emotionally, Johnson ponders how keying down his football personality might affect his game. Johnson knows there is a line he must walk. "How do you do that? I don't know. It would almost be like not caring. If you love this game the way I love it, that's why I'm so emotional," Johnson said, days after the Pittsburgh loss. "I guess that's something I can work on, to channel my energies somewhere else when things aren't going the right way."

It's the same dilemma he faced growing up. If he'd taken school seriously, Johnson's trip to NFL stardom would have been smoother. But would it have been as motivational?

"My grandmother's way for me—go to school, get the grades—was so much easier, but I didn't see it that way. I talk to kids all the time now. My message is always school. I held myself back by not going. I did it the hard way. If I could go back, I'd do it different. Sometimes I wonder, though. If I did it the right way, would I still be as hungry? Maybe that struggle was good. I don't think I'd be the same 85 if I did the four years of college."

Marvin Lewis, Hue Jackson and Charles Collins—those closest to him in the game—would like to see Johnson better recognize the impact he has on his teammates and on aspects of the game that don't involve him catching the ball. As Lewis said, "We have to make him aware of the other ten guys on defense, not just the player lined up across from him."

Collins, as befits his style, is more blunt. At halftime of the playoff game, Collins says he saw "the Santa Monica Chad."

"I will always keep him knocked down a peg....Everybody else is always praising him. Not me. That's not my job."—Hue Jackson

Collins' message to his star pupil is simple: "You've made the Pro Bowl. I'm waiting for you to be a professional.

"I'll know he's a professional when he starts making better decisions. It won't be about Chad. It'll be about winning and leading the team, not just in catches, but in character."

Something Johnson will not change is his loyalty to his friends in Miami, those who knew him growing up. "As fast as I got here, that's how fast it could be taken away. I always keep that in the back of my mind. What you see is what you get," he said. "That won't change."

It's a side of Johnson that worries his mother. Paula Johnson says the money and fame have brought people into her son's life

she'd have preferred would stay away. She's concerned enough, she says she will be happier when her son's football career is over.

"He wants to be a gangster," Paula Johnson says. "He wants that image, but that's not him," Paula says. She recalls Chad spending so much time at a Jewish Community Center in Miami that she once remarked, "what I really have is a little black Jewish boy."

"My mom raised him the way she raised me," says Paula Johnson. "She steered him away from the neighborhood."

Chad Johnson will say his mother is overreacting. And that even though he didn't spend a lot of time with his peers in Liberty City, he still knew them well from playing football against them growing up.

Paula Johnson fears the posse mentality sometimes fostered by athletes and entertainers could get her son in trouble. What can happen is, an athlete's close friends begin involving their friends in the athlete's life, and lifestyle. The connection spreads until the athlete no longer knows everyone who claims him as a friend. When the strangers claiming to be friends find trouble, the possibility exists they can involve the athlete in something he had nothing to do with.

"That's what you have to be careful with," says Bengals

coach Marvin Lewis. "The hangers-on. It's not even always the hangers-on. It's the hangers-on to the hangers-on."

Paula Johnson says that on her trips home to her mother's house, she has noticed "cars lined up. It's like a street parade out in front of my mother's house at one o'clock in the morning. He's inside, just sitting there.

"Chad looks at people one way. There are no bad guys to him. He's trusting. He doesn't know these guys. They claim to be friends of his. I don't like what's going on now. The football. I want it over. It's put a strain on our relationship. All these outsiders. What should be the happiest time in my life is one of the saddest times."

Marvin Lewis is less concerned. "Chad's posse is self-contained," the Bengals coach says. "No branches." Lewis says that Johnson's agent, Drew Rosenhaus, has told the coach that Johnson is his easiest client to deal with.

Paula Johnson hopes that as her son matures as a person, her worries will take care of themselves. For now, Chad Johnson's focus is so tightly engaged with football—and his personality away from the game so reticent—it seems implausible he'd be making headlines for anything other than playing the game.

Hue Jackson sees a very good wide receiver who wants to be great, and is willing to put in the needed time. He saw a different Johnson on the next-to-last Sunday of the regular season in 2005. The sight pleased the Bengals wide receivers coach.

The Bengals were playing the Buffalo Bills. Johnson was being covered much of the game by a Bills cornerback named Nate Clements. If Johnson had created a "Who Covered 85" List in 2004, Clements would have had his "Yes" box checked. He held Johnson to two catches for 10 yards in a December game the Bills won, 33-17. The loss knocked the Bengals from playoff contention. The following season, when the two teams met again, Johnson called himself "a man on a mission."

One thing Jackson had emphasized to Johnson was Johnson's need to improve running with the ball after the catch. "You always end up out of bounds or falling down," Jackson had told him. It was reminiscent of what Charles Collins and Craig Austin had said during Johnson's junior college days. "I told him he had to be aware of where the defender is after you catch the ball," said Jackson. "That comes from working at it, every day, having someone stay on you, making you understand that every time you catch the ball, you can score. This isn't just about running fast. That's not football."

During the season, no one has a bigger, daily influence on Johnson than Hue Jackson. Marvin Lewis says, "I hope I'm fatherly with him," and the coach is. But Lewis' reach has to extend further than his star wideout. The daily issues of Dealing With Chad don't fall to Lewis.

Jackson counsels Johnson not just because he cares for him, but to make him a better player. Jackson spends time getting to know all his wide receivers. It helps him know how to deal with each, individually. "I need to know what makes them tick. Guys will give you a little more if you take that extra time," Jackson explained.

As with Charles Collins before him, Johnson listens to Hue Jackson. Johnson has come to understand Jackson can help him become a better football player. Nothing means more to Chad Johnson than becoming a better football player.

"He allows me to coach him," Jackson says. Jackson's approach with Johnson might not be what you'd expect.
The next time Hue Jackson praises his star pupil will be the first. "He tells me I'm 365 degrees below fly shit," Johnson says.

"He's mean, man, but so father-like. He doesn't care about Pro

Bowls or trash-talking. He never praises me. Why should he praise me for doing what I'm supposed to do? I don't get praise. Not yet."

Says Jackson, "I'm never going to let him be bigger than he is. I will always keep him knocked down a peg. We're a lot alike. He's emotional. So am I. We butt heads, but we both want the same things. Everybody else is always praising him. Not me. That's not my job. There are times he thinks he's doing good when he isn't."

Even Jackson was pleased at what he saw during the 2005 game against Buffalo. "Nate Clements had always been one of his nemeses. Chad had something to prove. That day, he competed like I hadn't seen."

For Hue Jackson, the eye-opener was Johnson's 41-yard, catch-and-run touchdown across the middle, late in the first half. "I saw a new player emerge. He caught the ball and just kept running. That's the next step for him. He already has that mentality of 'You can't cover me.' The Chad Johnson who has a chance to be a great player takes that and adds, 'You can't tackle me. I'm scoring every play.' If he can do that, he can score 15 touchdowns, every year."

During the game, Johnson said to Jackson, "Coach, you created a tiger today. Every time I catch the ball, I'm going to the end zone."

"The light came on that day," Jackson said, a month after the game. The Bengals lost, 37-27, but Johnson caught nine passes, for 117 yards and the 41-yard TD. "His mentality was, 'I'm the best player on this field. Nate Clements is not going to stop me from blocking or catching and he's damned sure not going to keep me from running after the catch.'"

No one questions Johnson's dedication to his game. Everyone waits for the day when he funnels all of it the proper way. Being respected as a player isn't enough, if you aspire to greatness.

"Him realizing how important he is to the mental well-being

of the team," said Marvin Lewis, when asked what might be the next step in Johnson's evolution. "I don't think he understands the impact he has."

For all his on-camera flamboyance, candor and charm, there are days when Johnson's sunny personality finds a cloud. It occurs much more than the public sees. It's not predictable and, because Johnson is a star and a veteran and such a presence, it can affect his teammates. "That could be Wednesday or Thursday," said Lewis. "That could be Saturday morning after three great practices." Or halftime of the first Bengals playoff game in fifteen years.

"I'm not vocal in the locker room," Johnson insists. "I'm not a preacher." But if the most outspokenly confident member of the team suddenly stops being outspokenly confident, people begin to wonder. Even people inside the locker room.

"He puts in the effort. It's the fine points he needs to work on," Lewis said, a month after the '05 season. "When he takes all that passion and competitive fire and does what he needs to do consistently, all the time, when times are tough, when the game's on the line, to line up correctly, to run the (pass) route the way it was practiced. . . when he does that all the time, then we can say he's a great player."

Johnson grasps this. He listens. "I've come to understand ninety percent of the game is mental. Seeing the coverage before it happens. Seeing it unfold right before your eyes, and already knowing what to do. The sky's the limit if I can put the mental together with the physical," he said.

Meantime, Johnson will be Johnson. A public hoot, a world-class entertainer, still that people-loving, "straight-up clown" his Miami mentor Terrence Craig has known for twenty years. Also, the subdued little boy with lots of acquaintances but few close friends, who finds peace in the quiet of his grandmother's house, where he grew up.

He thinks he'd like to act. The camera is good to him. It captures his public essence: The smile, the clowning, the warmth. The ability to connect and feel at home with all kinds of people, forged during his years growing up in Miami, attending a series of racially diverse schools.

"I've got savvy for that camera," is how Johnson puts it. "You have to have a swagger about yourself. I don't need a script. I just go."

He spent some time the week before the '06 Super Bowl, working for the NFL Network, roaming the environs of the Renaissance Center in Detroit, conducting random interviews with players and fans. Johnson came off as particularly embraceable. He always has.

It's the same charm that kept him in high school football and out of detention. It's the same potential and ingratiating manner that inspired so many people to keep taking chances on him. It's what got him this far.

But TV is not football. So it has no place.

Not yet.

"I could do TV now, in the off-season, but I wouldn't have much time," Johnson said last February, barely a month after the playoff loss. "I'd have to be back in April for our off-season conditioning."

Hue Jackson has said this to Chad Johnson, more than once: "Life is what you carve out for yourself. When you have a closed fist, nothing can go out, nothing can come in. When you have an open hand, you get it going out and coming in."

Johnson's hand is always open. Because, to hear him tell it, he's always open.

7-11.

He can't be stopped.

After the Pittsburgh loss, among Chad Johnson's final words were these: "We're going to get back and finish this."

If he needed any more incentive, there was also this:

The 2007 Super Bowl would be played in Miami.

INDEX

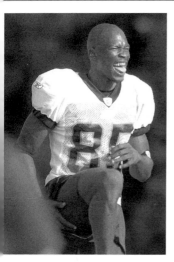

"Keyshawn is more the talking type. I'm more of a keep my mouth shut. I lead by example on the field."—Chad Johnson, speaking of himself and his cousin, NFL wide receiver Keyshawn Johnson, on April 22, 2001, the day the Cincinnati Bengals drafted him.

Paul Daugherty has been a sports columnist in Cincinnati since 1988. During that time, he has won numerous writing awards, including five top-five finishes in the Associated Press Sports Editors national contest. He has been named best sports columnist in Ohio five times and best general columnist once. A native of Washington, D.C., Paul lives in Loveland, Ohio, with his wife Kerry and their two children, Kelly and Jillian.